Confucianism

A SHORT INTRODUCTION

Confucianism

A SHORT INTRODUCTION

John H. and Evelyn Nagai Berthrong

ONEWORLD
OXFORD

CONFUCIANISM: A SHORT INTRODUCTION

Oneworld Publications
(Sales and Editorial)
185 Banbury Road
Oxford OX2 7AR
England
http: //www.oneworld-publications.com

Oneworld Publications
(US Marketing Office)
160 N Washington St.
4th Floor, Boston
MA 02114
USA

ISBN 1-85168-236-8

Cover design by Design Deluxe
Typeset by Saxon Graphics, Derby, UK
Printed and bound in England by Clays Ltd, St Ives plc

CONTENTS

ACKNOWLEDGEMENTS

Sometimes small books have many friends. It is certainly the case for this introduction to the Confucian tradition. There has been a renaissance of studies of various aspects of the Confucian tradition that now stretches back at least four decades in North America and Europe. As we view East Asia, we must remember the foundational work of a small group of Chinese scholars now known as the New Confucians. Their reflections began in the 1920s and 1930s when times seemed darkest for anyone seriously interested in the study of or commitment to Confucianism as a philosophic tradition and way of life. Along with this early cohort of the New Confucian movement, we must also acknowledge the fact that serious scholars have continued the study of Confucianism in Korea and Japan throughout the twentieth century and into the twenty-first century. It is upon the labors of these last four generations that this work is built.

There are more proximate groups of people we need to thank. We think especially of Wm. Theodore de Bary of Columbia University. He has provided continuous active leadership ever since 1950. Many of his students have gone on to become major scholars in the field as well. On the Chinese side we would be remiss not to mention teachers and colleagues such as Tu Weiming, Julia Ching, Cheng Chung-ying, and Liu Shu-hsien. In this group we also want to thank the Neo-Confucian Seminar of Columbia University. The Seminar has provided a venue over the years to test our ideas and to profit from the research of friends and colleagues from around the world.

Over the last five years a number of people have provided even more stimulation for this work, even if they were unaware of the role they would play in the writing of it. Our colleagues in the Confucian Studies Group of the American Academy of Religion and the Society for the Study of Chinese Religion (often active at the Association for Asian Studies) have helped to promote the cause of Confucian studies within the larger world of North America. Sometimes we even have the pleasure of welcoming friends from Asia and Europe. We add our thanks to colleagues such as Joseph Adler, Mary Evelyn Tucker, Deborah Summer, John Chaffee, Zheng Jiadong, John Henderson, Michael Nylan, P. J. Ivanhoe, Peter Bol, Zhang Longxi, Irene Bloom, Hoyt Tillman, Rodney Taylor, Lisa Raphals, Hal Roth, Peter Nosco, Janine Sawada, Roger Ames, David Hall, Chen Lai, Michael Kalton, Lionel Jensen, Thomas H. C. Lee, Mark Setton, and Philip Clart. We hope that all of these named and unnamed colleagues will recognize the good they have contributed and not notice where we have misused their diverse achievements.

At Boston University we thank Robert C. Neville, Joseph Fewsmith, Livia Kohn, David Eckel, Merle Goldman, Ray Hart, John Clayton, Peter Berger, Adam Seligman, Robert Weller, Chung Chai-sik, Wesley Wildman, and Jensine Andresen for their interest, correction, and conversation. We also want to thank our research assistant, Mr. He Xiang, and Ms. Tracy Deveau, a perfect administrative assistant. The university administration of Dennis Berkey, Provost, and Jon Westling, President, has provided generous support for and appreciation of scholarship and research. This support included a leave in 1999 that was instrumental in finishing the project.

Even closer to home, we need to thank our son, Sean Berthrong, and our good friend Loretta Cubberly, who could always be counted upon to look after the house as we traveled around the country and the world.

Our colleagues at Oneworld Publications, especially Victoria Warner, have given us constant encouragement all along the way. We owe an immense debt of gratitude to them for allowing us to write a different kind of introduction to a great philosophic and religious tradition.

Plate 1 *Guardian figures at the entrance to a temple in the Forest of Confucius, Qufu, the ancestral burial ground of the Kong family. The Forest includes a tumulus believed to have once held the remains of Confucius himself.* Photo: Evelyn Berthrong.

1 INTRODUCTORY REFLECTIONS

INTRODUCING CONFUCIAN LIVES

Confucianism has been and still is a vast, interconnected system of philosophies, ideas, rituals, practices, and habits of the heart that informs the lives of countless people in East Asia and now the whole inhabited world. Although known in the West mostly as a philosophic movement, Confucianism is better understood as a compelling assemblage of interlocking forms of life for generations of men and women in East Asia that encompassed all the possible domains of human concern. Confucianism, at various times and places, was a primordial religious sensibility and praxis; a philosophic exploration of the cosmos; an ethical system; an educational program; a complex of family and community rituals; dedication to government service; aesthetic criticism; a philosophy of history; the debates of economic reformers; the intellectual background for poets and painters; and much more. For instance, we owe to Confucians in East Asia the most extensive written historical record for any human civilization from its beginning down to today. We also owe Confucians medical prescriptions, vast hydraulic works, bonsai and wonderful gardens.

In China, Korea, Japan and Vietnam, Confucians historically created worldviews, ways of life, and deeply shared cultural orientations and sensibilities that are still alive today. Confucians paid attention to art, morality, religion, family life, science, philosophy, government, and the economy. In short, Confucians were profoundly concerned with all aspects of human life. Moreover, Confucians played a distinguished role in creating innovative reflections and achievements in all dimensions and endeavors of human life. The collected modalities form the tapestry of civilization. The Confucians have always had a complex, holistic and organized view of human life, nature, character, thought, and conduct. It is also a fascinating question to explore how Confucians understood their "culture," or Dao/Way as they called it, over long centuries and vast spaces.

We have created an iconic (and fictional) Confucian husband and wife, Dr. and Mrs. Li, living in the famous, cultivated, and beautiful city of Suzhou (situated in central China just south of the great Yangtze river) in 1685. The Lis are what is called an "ideal type" or prototype, a generalized portrait of what the lives of a late imperial Confucian couple might have been. We have chosen this method in order to make the point that Confucianism is so much more than the history of ideas. It was and is a complicated pattern of human life, which affected men and women differently. Furthermore, how they understood Confucianism depended on their social position: elite couples like the Lis could be self-consciously Confucian whereas a poor peasant family in the southeast of China might only have the faintest understanding of the teaching of the Confucian tradition. However, as we shall see, Confucianism touched the lives of all the peoples in East Asia. Of course, it formed the lives of such a prototypical couple as Dr. and Mrs. Li more closely and more richly in 1685 than anyone else in Chinese society. It is because of the richness and influence of such elite Confucian culture at the end of its grand imperial career that we have dared to resort to such a narrative strategy.

By choosing 1685, we will be viewing Confucian society in one of its more accomplished moments. The ruler was the great Kangxi emperor (1662–1723), who, although a Manchu noble from beyond the ethnic world of traditional China, was undoubtedly one of the most brilliant men ever to hold the throne. He was fascinated by the world around him and, from what we can tell, was dedicated to the just and harmonious rule of an expanding empire. Whatever his ultimate personal commitments, Kangxi was clearly interested and educated in the broad sweep of traditional Confucian culture. He also illustrates the fact that Confucianism was already a multicultural and international movement. The Confucian tradition itself was undergoing the effects of the development of the last great traditional Confucian philosophic movement, the justly famous school of Evidential Research. Though the Evidential Research scholars were critical of the philosophy of their Han, Song, Yuan, and Ming forefathers, they carried the scholarly aspects of Confucianism to new heights.

"Confucianism" is a Western term but everyone recognizes Confucius (551–479 B.C.E.) as the founder of the movement that takes his name. This would have struck Master Kong, to use his Chinese title and name, as suspect. Master Kong believed fervently that his role was to restore the way of the ancient sages rather than to propound some novel set of doctrines. However, as is so often the case with great religious and cultural reformers, the more they seek to renew the past, the more they generate a new culture out of the old. This is precisely what Master Kong achieved.

Master Kong had a grave problem. By his time, the Zhou dynasty was in obvious decline. Although the Warring States period would not begin until after his death, Master Kong's question was, how to revive the Zhou? His answer was simple: we need to study the history of the great Zhou founders in order to recover and restore the Chinese world.

A CONFUCIAN WORLD

Returning to the era of Dr. and Mrs. Li, by 1685 China (and other countries in East Asia) had been thoroughly steeped in Confucian culture for centuries. For instance, in 1313 the Mongol court declared one form of Confucian thought, namely the synthesis of Zhu Xi (1130–1200), the basis for the imperial examinations. The local, provincial, and national examination system was based on the Confucian classics and became more and more powerful in the later Ming and Qing dynasties. But this was not the only story. Along with formal education for the imperial examinations came many other Confucian influences in art, poetry, family life, and local social organization.

Late imperial China was a "Confucian" culture in the sense that intellectual concerns, moral axioms, education, family rituals, and political ideology all bore the marks of Confucian reflection and action. Confucianism permeated all levels of Chinese life. Even the classes that did not have access to formal Confucian education and social status firmly believed that if a family were to climb the ladder of success, Confucian education and culture were the only sure ways to move up the social scale. Of course, there were dissenters among Daoists and Buddhists, though even the learned clergy among these two alternative traditions also knew the Confucian classics as well as they did their own scriptures. The majority of the Chinese people were touched in almost every aspect of their lives by Confucian activities.

Was this vast Confucian influence on Chinese culture a good thing? This question cannot be answered with a simple yes or no. Most Confucians thought so; but sometimes the best and most critical Confucians harbored their own doubts. Had Confucianism lost its ethical edge? Had it become too rigid? Had it become too closely linked to an authoritarian state apparatus? Many modern Chinese, Korean, Japanese, Vietnamese, and Western critical scholars have blamed the late Confucian social system and imperial system for fossilizing East Asian culture in the name of the First Sage. The Confucian world became backward looking and fossilized. But was this really the case? This is another question with no simple answer. From the perspective of the 1920s, the veritable low point of modern Chinese history, the criticism of Confucianism seemed eminently justified. Like a ship's captain, the wreck of the Sinitic culture and the loss of respect for that cultural world happened on the Confucian watch. Something new was desperately needed to save China and the rest of East Asia.

Now, however, Confucianism shows signs of internal renewal and the remarkable contemporary economic success of East Asia is being linked to enduring Confucian values of love of education, respect for family, hard work, and the desire for a social order built on consensus and harmony rather than individual competition. What is Confucian and what is not in Chinese culture is another hard question to answer when so many things were defined as "Confucian." Nonetheless, it is accurate to say that Confucianism is one major aspect of a shared Chinese cultural sensibility. The Confucian Way lives on in complicated modalities in the people of East Asia and in the wider Asian Diaspora. Only time will tell what will happen to this great living cultural artifact.

INTERNATIONAL AND CROSS-CULTURAL CONFUCIANISM

Because of limitations of format and space, we cannot extend our discussion to the role of Confucianism in all the diverse countries of East Asia. This is a pity. Although in the West Confucianism is considered a prime marker of Chinese culture, Confucianism is an international religious and philosophic movement. It spread from China into Korea, Japan, and Vietnam. But Confucianism was more than just a borrowed morsel of Chinese cultural life, it became an active part in the lives of the Korean, Japanese, and Vietnamese people over the centuries. Moreover, it was creatively developed in unique ways in each new cultural situation.

Each East Asian country adapted Confucianism as part of the Chinese cultural package. The case of Korea is particularly fascinating. As the Korean state emerged, Confucianism became more and more important in Korean culture. By the end of the fourteenth century, the long-lived Choson dynasty (1396–1910) declared Confucianism to be the orthodox philosophy (and religion) of Korea. In the centuries that followed, Korean scholars appropriated and refined the Neo-Confucian tradition. It is not an exaggeration to say that the best philosophic work of the sixteenth century in East Asia was done in Korea. No one advanced the specifics of Zhu Xi's synthesis more than the Koreans. Moreover, the Koreans even drastically transformed their family structure, including marriage ritual, to conform to orthodox Confucian models. The Koreans could say without fear of contradiction that by the eighteenth century they were the most Confucian country in East Asia.

Confucianism spread to Japan after it was introduced in Korea. In the early part of Japanese history, Confucianism was taught in Buddhist monasteries as part of the general education fit for the aristocracy. Since the Tang period (618–907) in China, the Japanese were highly impressed with all aspects of Chinese culture, although it was Buddhism that was more important spiritually and culturally. But with the rise of the Tokugawa (1600–1868) shoguns, Confucianism played an increasingly important role in Japanese culture. The shoguns made use of Confucian statecraft and Japanese intellectuals became as fascinated by the philosophical and historical intricacies of Confucian thought as were their Chinese and Korean cousins. By the seventeenth and eighteenth centuries, as in Korea, Japanese scholars were expanding the range of Confucian thought in new directions. At the end of the Tokugawa period, for instance, many of the young reformers who carried out the great Meiji (1868) reforms, were inspired by an activist vision of Confucian social morality. Even today Confucianism contributes to the unique mix of modern Japanese culture.

We know much less about the role of Confucianism in Vietnam save for the fact that the kings and scholars of Vietnam also imported Confucian texts as part of their general appreciation of Chinese elite culture.

Confucianism, perhaps less so than in either Korea or Japan, also plays a role in the modern life of Vietnam.

Both Korea and Japan are fascinating modern societies. They are industrial powers, as modern as any countries in the world. They are now also robust democratic societies, the roles of women are changing rapidly in both societies, yet Confucian culture continues to play a role in the lives of their people. One point illustrates the continuing role of Confucian thought. Traditionally, descent was through the male line in a Chinese family for ritual purposes. However, with smaller and smaller families, sometimes with a single daughter, the Chinese have kept the style from former times in terms of family shrines, but now will cheerfully place a daughter where a son would have gone traditionally. Times change but Confucian sensitivities continue to play a remarkably persistent and complex role in the life of East Asia.

We will return to the history of Confucian thought in the chapter on Dr. Li's lecture to the academy on the theme of Confucian history and in the chapter on Confucian teachings. However, the two presentations will be different. The chapter on Confucian teachings is what is called an etic history and the second, Dr. Li's lecture, is called an emic account. The terms "etic" and "emic" are taken from anthropology; the former refers to an external telling of the tale, the latter to an internal one. We have tried to write Dr. Li's lecture in an emic style, in the way a late Qing literatus Confucian would have told the story. But emic accounts assume that their audience already knows a great deal about the story. Dr. Li is lecturing serious young men who have been studying Chinese thought for around twenty years before they arrive at the academy. Conversely, an etic narration sees other things that might be overlooked because they are so commonplace to an emic scholar. There is value in both, and a balance of etic and emic narrations of the story will help a new audience better understand the contours of the Confucian Way.

A LIVING TRADITION

It is vital to understand that Confucianism is a living religion and a way of cultural formation: its religious dimension is accompanied by philosophy, ritual theory, historical studies, poetic craft, the arts of calligraphy and painting, and political ideology as well. All of these form what we call the Confucian Way. The Confucian Way is a total way of life within the East Asian world. This is one of the reasons that many modern East

Asian people pause when they are asked about their "religion." They understand this question to mean, are they a "member" of a specific religious tradition in the manner of Judaism, Christianity, or Islam. Because Confucianism is organized and understood differently from the great religious traditions of the West and Middle East, many East Asians will pause and say that they have no religion because Confucianism has never been defined as religion with initiation or membership (i.e., you are not initiated into Confucianism in the ways common to the religions of the West). But ask a second question (suggested insightfully by Jordan Paper), to whom do you owe sacrifice? The answer will be completely different. The question of family ritual and sacrifice, as we shall see, cuts to the heart of the religious dimension of the Confucian Way.

Confucianism has always been linked to a classical education, and education in traditional China was the mark of elite culture. Confucianism, therefore, has always been seen as the domain of China's cultural, economic, and political elites. This is true again to a certain extent. However, because of its leading social role in Chinese society, Confucianism was more and more attractive to all levels of the expanding Chinese cultural world. One of our arguments is that this was a complex problem, and Confucianism's success was merited by its intrinsic impetus. One of the lessons of Chinese history is that no one, not even a supremely powerful emperor such as the great first founder of the unified imperial state, Qin Shi Huangdi, could impose an ideology upon the population if those people do not accept it in their mind-hearts. More and more through the long history of China Confucian thought and practice suffused all levels and domains of Chinese life, and later, the lives of the people of Korea, Japan, and Vietnam as well.

Confucianism rests, as do all the various paths or religions of China, on the cultural foundations of the sinitic world. Confucianism is one major expression of the genius of Chinese cultural sensibilities. Modern scholarship suggests that the Confucian impact on Chinese culture can be divided into three different modalities. Confucianism was first a particular popular form of pan-Chinese thought and practice; in fact, Confucianism represented itself as the epitome of classical Chinese culture. We call this popular Confucianism. The second form consists of the uses made by the various dynasties of China of Confucians in order to rule China and to create an ideology that relied on Confucian themes for its justification. This is imperial, political, or ideological Confucianism. The third can be labeled reform Confucianism. This is the Confucianism of

reforming intellectuals who took their Confucian thought very seriously
as a way to renew or reform the Chinese cultural world. All three forms
of Confucianism interacted with each other, and oftentimes it is hard to
distinguish one form from another.

CULTURAL CONCERNS

Merely to describe the intellectual history of Confucianism, a worthy
enterprise from the Confucian point of view, misses much about the lives
of ordinary and extraordinary Confucians over the centuries. No single
academic disciplinary approach covers all that needs to be presented in
order to introduce the Confucian world to people living beyond its home
in East Asia. We need a mixture of art history, ethics, religious theory, philosophy, science, political science, and economics just to begin the project.

Dr. and Mrs. Li are in early middle age; he is in the early 40s and she
is in her early 30s. Dr. Li is an official of the Qing dynasty serving as a
local magistrate in the beautiful garden city of Suzhou. Mrs. Li is his first
wife and mother of four children, two boys and two girls. She is also an
accomplished poet in various forms of classical Chinese genres. Our fictional couple is what the great German sociologist Max Weber would
have called an "ideal type." Another way to see this social construction
of reality is to call the Lis a prototype following contemporary metaphor
theory. Metaphor and prototype theory says that we have favorite cultural and linguistic models, such as the robin being the perfect image of
a bird for English speakers.

The Lis are a composite family we have invented so as to introduce
the diverse aspects of Confucian life. In order to provide such a portrait,
it is important to include Confucian women, as well as men. As we shall
see, Mrs. Li plays a very important role not only in her family but also
in the larger cultural world of late imperial China. Educated Confucian
women took on the crucial task of first teacher for their children; they
also took part in the major festivals and rituals that defined the passage
of time during the year and the entire life cycle.

This very short description already tells us a great deal about Dr. and
Mrs. Li. For instance, we know that they are part of China's ruling elite,
often called the literati class. Furthermore, we know that Dr. Li is part of
an elite within an elite. Because of his administrative rank and age, we
surmise, correctly, that he has passed all three of the grueling local,
provincial, and national examinations that are the prerequisite of entry

into the imperial civil service. Mrs. Li's exquisitely crafted classical poetry demonstrates that she is a daughter of an elite family as well; a family of scholars and officials as the Chinese would say.

Dr. and Mrs. Li take their roles as educators very seriously. Dr. Li is not only an imperial civil servant; he is a guardian of what Confucians call "this culture of ours." His responsibility is to serve in the larger world of politics, education, economics, law, and even military affairs. He serves his emperor but also bears the weight of a tradition that demands his critical evaluation of the dynasty that he serves. Dr. Li is not a mere careerist seeking a salary. Mrs. Li's world is defined as the inner chambers of her home; she runs the family just as Dr. Li serves in the civil service. She bears the responsibility for the functioning of the elaborate compound of a Qing official. Moreover, she is profoundly aware of her duties as an educated woman to introduce her children to their first steps on the path to Confucian self-cultivation.

Living in Suzhou during this period also places the Lis in the midst of one of the most beautiful cities in the heart of early Qing culture. There is a Chinese saying that goes, "Heaven above, Suzhou and Hangzhou below." It is at the center of the Chinese intellectual world; it is also a city some have called the Venice of the East. Critics might counter that we are painting a much too positive view of Confucian life. That comment does have merit, but we will point out problems with the tradition as well. Mrs. Li, for instance, suffers from bound feet as do her young daughters, as well as a lack of general access to the world beyond her home.

We have chosen to present the tradition at its best. Intercultural comparisons often follow an apple and orange approach; the best and most noble ideals of one culture are compared and contrasted to the worst practices of another culture. We are seeking to present a picture of Confucian lives and culture at its best so that they can be compared to the ideals of other cultures. Of course, no culture lives up to its ideals. Dr. and Mrs. Li know this all too well.

CONFUCIANISM AS A WAY OF LIFE

Confucianism was a whole way of life. It was an ideology; it was rituals and social customs; it was an education curriculum; it did have spiritual dimensions; it did have strong philosophic opinions. Confucianism was both good and bad. The best Confucians commended the good and struggled to reform the bad done in its name. It is a commonplace in the study of religion to observe that religion brings forth the best and the worst of human behavior. Nothing is more savage than people going forth convinced that God or the Dao is on their side. But then, nothing restrains such atavistic self-conceits more than the teachings of religion about respect for other persons and love of neighbors. Confucianism is just like any other religion or comprehensive worldview in this regard.

Confucians considered themselves the epitome of all the other forms of Chinese cultural expression. Although Confucians, as a ruling elite, were remarkably tolerant of the other traditions, this did not mean that they were unaware of the profound differences between and among them. The most basic point that Confucians defended against the other philosophic and religious perspectives was a strong realistic sense of the concrete nature of the world. Confucians were and are realists. They defended their "culture" as a "real" or "solid" tradition. By this they meant, philosophically, that the world of objects and events is real and independent of the mentality and wishes of human beings. Even the great mystics of the tradition, such as Wang Yangming (1472–1529), had a robust respect for the world. The Confucians contrasted their world-view with the Daoist claims about vacuity and the Buddhist preaching about emptiness. Moreover, as an elite tradition, the literati Confucians heaped scorn or condescension upon the folk religion of the common people. Although Confucians would rarely try to suppress folk beliefs (unless they became politically dangerous in their eyes), they tried to educate the common people into taking a more "realistic" Confucian view of reality.

The social claim the Confucians defended is that their tradition was based on the primordial learnings of family life. The ultimate warrant for the Confucian claim to "real" teachings rested on the social framework of the Confucian teachings that cultivated and educated the person from the cradle to the grave. Confucians considered themselves masters of the mundane world. And they would ask, what other world do we have? Their not so subtle point is that we do not have any other world. What-ever wonderful things the alchemy of the Daoists can offer, whatever bliss Buddhist meditation promises, we still have to raise our children and bury our parents. The rest is art.

On the other hand, it was hard for Daoists and Buddhists to dislike the Confucians with any intensity. The Confucians tried hard to be good and decent people so that about the best (or worst) that could be done to them was to be made fun of for being boring pedants. The Daoist master Zhuangzi (*c.* fourth century B.C.E.) had a genius for amusement at the expense of the Confucians, and often made Confucius sound like a Daoist. The Confucians tried to reform themselves and the world and usually ended up failing at both. Yet there was something noble about the attempt. As the Confucians said, someone had to mind the store of the world. We could not all be hermits and mad poets singing and drinking wine in the mountains in the fall. Someone had to make the wine, ship the wine, tax the wine, make sure that the wine was healthy for general consumption, and so forth. All this is mundane, but still, the Confucians pointed out that someone had to do it. Moreover, the Confucians were not so sure that there was no nobility in the mundane, or that the secular is not sacred.

Why was Confucianism so successful? Greece and Rome are only memories for the West although they live on in classical literature and works of art and architecture. The Middle Ages are dimly remembered. But China endures as a coherent culture from the Shang Dynasty to a modern and reforming industrial commercial giant. Confucianism played a major role in this story. Our argument will be that its success was due in part to the genius of the tradition. Was it always good? No. Was it always evil? Hardly. It was, as we shall see, a grand experiment built upon a unique and compelling vision of what it means to be human.

The classical period for the development of the tradition began with Confucius, though he would not have thought of himself as the founder of a new movement. Like many of the other great progenitors of a major spiritual path (Moses, Jesus, Mohammed, and the Buddha come to mind), Confucius thought of himself as reviving what was already the truth. From Confucius' perspective he was teaching about the wisdom of the former sages and worthies. In particular, Confucius focused his attention on the founding figures of the Zhou dynasty, namely King Wen, King Wu, and the Duke of Zhou. They were Confucius' historical models of what true culture should be about.

Confucius (Kongzi or Master Kong) believed that there was a long history of true teachings before his time as preserved in the records of the sage kings. He chose the early Zhou kings because he thought that their teachings were based on sound historical warrants. In addition, the Zhou founders, as sages and worthies themselves, had been able to build on the work of the teachings and models of the even earlier sage kings and worthies. The Zhou, therefore, amounted to a splendid summary of what culture ought to be. The moral actions and character of the early Zhou rulers were exemplars for anyone who aspired to virtue. In this regard, Confucius could honestly say that he was a transmitter of ancient culture and not some purveyor of modern vagaries.

Confucius' aim was to teach about the wisdom of the former sages, with the goal of reforming society. This reformation has a definite tone to it. Among all of Confucius' great axioms, the virtue of *ren* or humaneness stands out. Although *ren* was an old aristocratic virtue, Confucius gave it new life and a set of extended meanings. Before the Teachers of the Ages, *ren* meant something like *noblesse oblige* as the quality of care that a great noble owed to those in his charge. Confucius, self-consciously or not, expanded what had been a virtue based on aristocratic rank to the virtue of virtues in the Confucian world. Kongzi also made the radical suggestion that anyone could cultivate this virtue. Humaneness no longer depended on the accident of birth but rather on the commitment to cultivating a humane life.

Along with empathy and a strong sense of reciprocity, Confucius made humaneness operational for commoners as well as the sons of the Zhou aristocracy. Some of his students were aristocrats, but others, including his favorite student Yan Hui, were commoners. This was one of the most dramatic things that Master Kong and the Confucians ever did. They extended education, at least in theory, to anyone who wanted to learn. When the Master was asked if he was a sage or worthy, he stated clearly that he was not a sage or worthy, nor had he ever met any living sages or worthies. What could Confucius claim for himself if not the possession of his beloved list of revived classical virtues? He claimed only that he had never discovered anyone who loved learning more than he did. He did not assert that he knew more or even was a better student; Confucius only believed that he sincerely loved to learn, and what he loved to learn was the path of virtue. As he said, if you could hear the Dao/Way in the morning, you could die content on the very same evening. He meant that if you were able to embrace and embody the Dao as the way of the sages and worthies, what else could you want from life?

Whether Confucius was a conservative or radical social reformer is another question that we will never be able to answer, but he did inspire the *ru* or ritual specialists of his day to carry on the educational task he began. After his death his disciples continued teaching; but soon different schools emerged, each emphasizing different aspects of Confucius' teachings. In some cases, the reactions were so violent that the new teachers distanced themselves from the *ru* tradition completely.

The second of the great masters is Mengzi/Mencius (fl. fourth century B.C.E.) – and he is often known as the Second Sage. His was a more complicated intellectual landscape. Along with the growing Confucian tradition, there were many other schools vying for attention in the marketplace of ideas. The wars that would eventually lead to the unification of China were increasing in ferocity. Larger and more powerful states were now conquering the smaller ones. The rulers of the time were looking for effective advice on the part of philosophers about how to govern well and survive in difficult times. In fact, the issue of how to live in a time of political chaos was also a question that many philosophers were asking on behalf of individuals as well as the local governments. Many solutions were being offered.

Mencius strove to defend the Confucian Way against the other options of his time. The forces ranged against Mencius varied greatly. On the one extreme were the schools later called Legalists, who sought power, not virtue. They argued that only by understanding the uses of political power, a highly organized bureaucracy, and an autocratic legal system could the state flourish. Virtue was a waste of time; people really responded to pain and pleasure, which ought to be controlled by the state in terms of positive and negative laws. At the other end of the spectrum were the Daoists who said that the answer to the problem was simple – non-action or dropping out of the race for power altogether. The Daoists strove to live a life beyond the range of Confucian social concerns. In the middle were thinkers like Yang Zhu, who rejected politics and posited a way of life devoted to survival. And of course, there was Mozi and his followers who sought social reform by teaching a utilitarian and pacifist vision for a peaceful society.

Mencius said all these people were wrong. They missed the point by not understanding the way of the sages and worthies. Only the teachings of the Confucian school were balanced enough between and among all the options to provide a sure philosophic and political program for reform. Like the other philosophers of his day, Mencius made his living by giving advice to rulers. In giving this advice, he built upon the early teachings of Confucius and expanded the message in sophisticated ways. For instance, Mencius was keen to show how the state could be reformed based on his analysis of human nature and its proper cultivation. He explained that all people have what he called the seeds of virtue. What they needed to do was to nurture these seeds by cultivating their mind-heart. The ruler was no exception. If the ruler could cultivate the Confucian virtues, then he would draw others to him by example and by a refined ethical form of statecraft.

The arguments continued after Mencius' death and became even more complicated. Just before the final unification by the Qin first emperor, another great Confucian arose to expound and defend the way of the sages. This was Xunzi (fl. fourth to third centuries B.C.E.). He became a controversial figure because of his famous argument with Mencius about human nature. Mencius had stated that human nature was ultimately good. Xunzi disagreed and held that human nature was evil or deformed. If this were the case, why was Xunzi even considered a Confucian? Xunzi believed that we could change the evil into good through a rigorous form of self-cultivation. This is where Xunzi's real debate with Mencius was played out. Xunzi believed that Mencius relied too much on the mind-heart being able to reform itself. Xunzi devised a complicated alternative form of education based on the Confucian understanding of ritual. He made the point that we could reform ourselves, but this needed a form of education based on the classical teachings of the sages and worthies.

Xunzi was also famous for writing articulate and sophisticated philosophic essays. He was able to defend Confucianism because he was a master of philosophic argumentation. He would patiently outline his case and show where the other schools were wrong. Xunzi insisted that the other philosophers failed because they were one-sided. According to Xunzi, the great Daoist Zhuangzi knew wonderfully the mystic ways of the cosmic Dao but not the ordinary functioning of daily life. The Legalist mastered the rule of law but failed to comprehend the role of ritual or civility as an essential aspect of social order. Although Xunzi created controversy for saying that Mencius was wrong about human nature, he was admired for the cogency of his Confucian philosophic vision and the clarity of his thought.

The second of the great periods of Confucian thought was the Han dynasty. Han Confucians had a doubly difficult task. In the first place, how could they compete with the great trio of Confucius, Mencius, and Xunzi? For the most part they did not, and developed other strategies for their work. Second, they arrived on the scene after the great intellectual disasters caused by Qin policy and the civil wars that raged before the Han rulers successfully reunited China. The Qin dynasty was very draconian about what books and schools it would allow. It banned, among others, the teachings of the Confucians and tried to destroy their precious books. Many works were completely lost.

When the Han dynasty reunited the country in the early second century B.C.E., they eventually decided to make Confucianism the official philosophy of the state. There were a number of reasons for this success. The Confucians restated the point that Xunzi had maintained, namely that they offered the most balanced form of social theory to be found. The Legalists were completely discredited, and the Han Confucians were subtle enough to incorporate elements from other schools in order to provide a comprehensive vision of the family, state, and world. The great Dong Zhongshu (second century B.C.E.) did this by grafting cosmological and philosophic theories onto the robust Confucian sense of social and personal ethics. Dong and the other Han Confucians created the synthetic style of Confucian thought that would dominate the Chinese world up to the end of the imperial era.

The next thing the Han Confucians did was to rescue as many lost and fragmented texts as possible. Although they were not completely successful in restoring all the lost texts, they did a magnificent job at editing the pre-Han texts from the Warring States period. All the texts that we now read, save for those discovered by recent archaeology, passed through the loving hands of the Han editors. Chinese culture owes a huge debt to their labors. Along with restoring the texts as best they could, the Han Confucians also continued the role of commentator. In fact, they are most often famous for writing lengthy commentaries in various modes on the classical texts. They began the practice of writing philosophy via commentary on the ancient texts. In this respect they were a great deal like Jewish, Christian, and Muslim theologians who sought to explain their visions by means of commenting on the texts of their traditions. After the Han period, commentary became the most revered way for a scholar to add to Confucian cultural history.

Han is also celebrated for its great historians. Confucianism has always placed great emphasis on history because it contained the records of the sages and worthies. There were historical documents before the Han, but it was the Han historians who gave shape to a historical tradition that survives until today. The grandest of the grand historians were the father and son combination of Sima Tan and Sima Qian (writing between 140 and 100 B.C.E.). Together they completed the *Records of the Grand Historian*, a comprehensive survey of Chinese history from its mythical beginnings to the Han dynasty. In the later part of the Han, the brother and sister team of Ban Gu and Ban Zhao wrote a history of the early Han dynasty. The Bans provided the model for the dynastic histories that continue to be written today. Along with the Han Confucian philosophers, the Han historians shaped how we understand the classical period of Chinese history.

By the end of the Han all the elements, at least in prototype, were in place for the development of the Confucian Way. The resources of the three great classical masters provided inspiration for future generations. Smaller texts such as the *Classic of Filial Piety*, the *Doctrine of the Mean*, and the *Great Learning* supplemented the insights of Confucius, Mencius, and Xunzi. Overarching all of these profoundly humanist and religious texts was the *Classic of Changes* functioning as a repository of the most profound teachings of the most ancient sages and worthies.

One of the main convictions of the Han Confucians was the essential unity of the cosmos. As they put it, there was a resonance and unity between and among heaven, earth, and humanity. Yet there was nothing final or finished about this unified cosmic vision. Confucians have always been fond of quoting the *Classic of Changes* to the effect that the Way of the cosmos is ceaseless production, generative creativity. In later versions, this vision of the endless fecundity of the cosmos developed into a realistic pluralism. Even when later Confucians seemed to defend a monistic view of the world, their cosmology depended on the reality of the various things, objects, and events of the world as real and not as illusory.

Rotating the lens on the elements of Han cosmology, a different order for the Confucian Way was generated out of the "things close at hand" as Confucians were apt to say. We start with the formation of the self, the cultivation of the moral seeds of virtue by intelligence, civility, compassion, empathy, and faithfulness to our true humanity. We begin with the person, but the person is never an isolated, unconnected individual. Rather, the person begins her or his nurture within a family context. It is the family that forms us from the cradle to the grave. Although Confucians placed great emphasis on the family and its potential virtues, they were well aware that not all families were wonderful or perfect places for the cultivation of virtuous persons. There are wonderful stories in the classics about great sages who had terrible parents. There are even stories of these same sages using mild deception on a father because they believed that they were serving an ideal image of a parent rather than the sorry example fate had dealt them in the flesh.

One of the most suggestive ways to characterize this Confucian theory of moral cultivation is to call it a form of concerned consciousness. From the Confucian point of view, all human life is directed by various forms of preconscious, unconscious, and conscious intentionality. There is a vector factor in all humanity leading to flourishing or floundering. We all have a choice, and we are universally *concerned* about the outcomes of our thoughts, intentions, and actions. We are not always successful; we are not always virtuous; but we are always concerned. Of course, this is a vast claim. A counterargument could be and was made that some people were not concerned about cultivating virtue in themselves – or in anyone else for that matter.

The Confucians reasoned that it was within the person and the family that we began our common quest for human integrity. However, they were not satisfied with stopping with the family. Although the family loomed large for Confucian thought, there was another imperative to move beyond the family circle and to extend the virtues found there into the wider ambit of the world at large. A cultivated person needed to live civilly with her or his neighbors and beyond the confines of the immediate community, into the world of the state and governance. Last, but not least, Confucians must learn to extend this concern for virtue to the farthest reaches of nature and the cosmos.

One of Mencius' most famous stories made the point perfectly. Mencius told the sad tale of Ox Mountain to show how nature mirrors human self-cultivation. Ox Mountain had once been a beautiful place, full of trees and wildlife. But after all the trees had been stripped from its sides, Ox Mountain became an ugly, useless lump, a desolate place not fit for animal or human habitation. Mencius drew the analogy with human nature. Was a deformed human nature the natural outcome of life? Yes and no. If human nature were cultivated correctly, then the natural outcome was a human life of humane flourishing and civil harmony. However, if destructive choices were made, then a person could fashion a life as ugly as Ox Mountain had become. Later, Xunzi, who argued with Mencius about many things, extended the argument by stating that our environments play a crucial role in the cultivation of virtue. Left to our own devices, Xunzi opined, human beings would too often turn themselves into personal versions of the desecrated Ox Mountain. That is why we need good teachings and teachers in order to provide a civil order capable of nurturing human flourishing.

According to the Confucian teachings, human beings must take responsibility for the whole created order. Of course, human beings are subject to the natural fluctuations of heaven and earth just as are all the other creatures, but we are responsible for what we make of our persons and our communities. The Song dynasty Confucians argued that a true person should be the first to worry about the trials and tribulations of the world and the last to enjoy its pleasures. Pleasure was not denied, but pleasure must be balanced against the need for a constant, intelligent concern for self and others. The end is a world at harmony.

The task was to assist the mind-heart, the center of the human person, to broaden and deepen its connection with heaven, the family, and the world. This is an arduous task, and that is why Confucians taught that the true Way of humanity and humaneness was long and the burden of true human culture was heavy. Further, once one task was accomplished, another loomed up. The reason for this was the fact that the world never stood still; reality was constantly changing, growing, dying, transforming itself and the human beings living within its cease-lessly creative processes. The trick of self-cultivation was to balance all these concerns so that the result was harmony and peace.

Self-cultivation was necessary to deepen the humane person, to imbue the mind-heart with the basic human virtues as expounded by the great sages and worthies. But merely enlarging the moral sensitivity of the person was not enough. It must be matched by a broadened concern for the family, society, the state, the international community, nature, and the cosmos itself. The ultimate task was and is to expand and develop the person's mind-heart into a life of humane concern and consciousness of the welfare of all humanity, and beyond humanity, to the entire world. It was a great task, yet it was also a joyful one when contemplated in all its glory. Had not Confucius said that to hear the Way in the morning and then die in the evening was fine because to embody the Way even for a moment was a grand and wonderful achievement?

By the second century C.E. the great Han dynasty was in terminal decay. With its fall, the first two eras of the Confucian Way were over. In many respects, the fall of the Han was like the fall of the Roman empire. Both marked the end of classical civilization. When the empire was finally reunited effectively in the seventh century, the world had changed forever. With the fall of the Han came the revival of Daoism and the arrival of Buddhism in China. The story of Chinese philosophy and religion from the third to the seventh centuries is the history of the incorporation of Buddhism into all aspects of Chinese life.

It is impossible to tell the complete story of how Buddhism impacted Confucian thought. Buddhism was, until the arrival of the Western powers in the nineteenth century, the first foreign high culture that the Chinese world had ever encountered. The Chinese were entranced by the beauty and profundity of the Buddhist dharma or teachings. By the time of the founding of the great Tang empire in 618, Buddhism had permeated every aspect of Chinese life, save for political theory, which remained solidly in Confucian hands. In fact, some scholars maintain that the period from the fall of the Han (*c.* 220) to the middle of the Tang (*c.* 740s) is actually a separate, medieval period for Confucianism. There is merit to this view. But another way to describe this period is to see it as something of a continuation of the age of commentary begun with the Han; the point here is that nothing terribly new or exciting was added to the Confucian repertoire during this long hiatus till the revival that began in the ninth century.

Confucianism never disappeared as a matter of intellectual concern nor lost its grip on vital sectors of the Chinese world during the peaceful Buddhist conquest of Chinese civilization. For instance, Confucian scholars continued their great work of commenting on their beloved classics. Confucians also continued to shape family ritual and the veneration of the ancestors as well as to staff the various civil services of the numerous successor states to the fallen Han empire. However, the most brilliant philosophic and religious minds were working on Buddhist problems and Buddhist teachings. These teachings would have a great deal of influence on later Confucian thought.

The third era arrives with the revival, in the Song dynasty (960–1279), of Confucianism, known in modern ecumenical scholarship as Neo-Confucianism. Traditionally, and someone like Dr. Li would follow the Song theorists in this regard, the beginning of the revival was dated to the Northern Song in the 1020s and afterward. However, when we look dispassionately at the historical record, it is clear that the philosophic revival began in the early part of the ninth century. By the Northern Song period, the renewal was underway with great strength and creativity. In Confucian eyes, this is another resurgent period of Confucian thought, second only to the founding works of the Zhou dynasty, and certainly more important than the work of the Han and Tang Confucians. Zhu Xi, looking back from the twelfth century at the genius of these Northern Song masters (*c.* 1020–1107), declared this to be a veritable rediscovery of the Confucian Way.

Zhu Xi's insight was that the Confucian Way in its full richness had been essentially lost or had gone underground ever since the time of Mencius. Of course, Zhu Xi recognized the great Han and Tang thinkers as Confucians, but with a difference. After Mencius, no one had access to the fullness of the Confucian vision. This changed dramatically, according to Zhu, with the work of his favorite four Northern Song masters. While we do not need to follow Zhu in all the twists and turns of his own philosophy of history, his point is still a good one. Things did change dramatically after the Northern Song. What most modern scholars now accept is a mid-Tang trickle followed by a Northern Song flood. Moreover, this spate of Confucian thinking was not confined to Zhu Xi's four Northern Song masters: it was the joint achievement of many different Confucian thinkers, from prime ministers to recluse scholars. The result was the grand new world of Neo-Confucian thought. Because someone like Dr. Li would have to know the history of Song thought thoroughly and would teach this history to his students, we will not go into very much detail concerning the evolutionary twists and turns of Confucian thought from the Song to the Qing. This history will be covered in Chapter 4 (Transmitting the Dao). From the perspective of Neo-Confucian thinkers, what began in the Northern Song, came to fruition with Zhu Xi, was challenged by Wang Yangming in the Ming, and recast in the Qing, was a single chain of intellectual history.

The Qing period represents a summation of traditional Confucian thought – either the fourth major period or a continuation of the Neo-Confucian age. All the major schools inherited from the Song and Ming had adherents in this period. There was a tremendous amount of work done on the history of Confucian thought. New editions of the great philosophers were published; moreover, there was a critical reaction to Song and Ming philosophy. The most vibrant Confucians of the Qing era wondered whether or not the Song and Ming had been too much influenced by strains of Buddhist thought. These Evidential Research scholars argued that Confucians must return to a more careful philological and historical study of Chinese history. In fact, one of the glories of the Qing period was the crafted work in philology, textual criticism, and history writing and theory. In the Qing, both Zhu Xi and Wang Yangming were challenged by new trends in the world of scholarship.

The fifth period begins in the 1840s with the arrival in force of the modern Western powers on the borders of China. At the time this would not have been perceived as anything beyond a minor barbarian irritation. However, history would prove that it was more than a minor skin blemish on the body of China. Coupled with the decline of the Qing dynasty, the relentless attacks of the Western powers caused the dramatic fall of imperial Confucian China. For a while it looked as if Confucianism were dead. If the fall of the Qing and the dismantling of Confucian status and privilege were not enough, surely the communist victory in 1949 spelled the death knell of the Chinese Confucian world. And if the communist victory in 1949 was insufficient, Mao's cultural revolution in the 1960s would finish off any lingering remains of Confucian sensibilities.

Nonetheless, the reports of the death of Confucianism have proved premature. Actually, from the 1920s on there was a group of Confucian scholars bent on reforming the tradition. They were not oblivious to the social and intellectual problems of the empire that was China and were often some of the strongest critics of a very moribund late imperial Confucianism. These Confucian reformers argued that there was a core or essence of the tradition that was worth saving. These scholars in China and the Chinese diaspora became known as the New Confucians. The New Confucians have now produced three full generations of thoughtful reformers of the tradition. In China today there are national and international Confucian associations. All this would have seemed impossible during the rampages of the cultural revolution. Even the New Confucians are not sure what to make of their tradition. Tu Weiming, the best known of the diaspora New Confucians, calls it the Third Wave of Confucianism. Tu believes that the first wave was the classical period and the second wave was the great revival in the Song, Yuan, Ming, and Qing periods. We are now witnessing the third wave. What makes this an exciting period for Confucian thought is the contact with the vitality of Western cultural forms. The only time this happened before was with the arrival of Buddhism, which led to an immense enrichment of the Confucian Way. The contact with Western philosophy and religion will surely have a great impact on Confucianism, and vice versa.

As we have pointed out before, Confucianism is already an international movement. The vicissitudes of Confucianism in the modern world have been different in each country in East Asia. In Korea, as in China, Confucianism was disestablished with the fall of the traditional Korean state in the late nineteenth and early twentieth centuries. Korea also suffered the indignity of becoming a colony of Japan in 1910 and did not regain its freedom till 1945. In Japan, the case is again different because

Confucianism was never as entrenched as it was in China or Korea. Although the Tokugawa shogunate (1600–1868) used Confucianism as part of its state ideology, it was never the sole official orthodoxy as it was in Korea and China. Vietnam also appropriated Confucianism, but appears to have responded more like Japan than China or Korea. Vietnam also suffered from becoming a French colony in the nineteenth century. In the cases of Korea, Japan, and Vietnam, Confucianism continues to play a role as a form of cultural DNA in the lives of these diverse people.

Confucianism has gone from being a state ideology to a nadir and then on to a significant renewal, all in one century. The religious and spiritual dimension of Confucianism continues to infuse the life of East Asian people and is now moving beyond the Pacific Rim to the Americas and Europe. It is truly an exciting time to contemplate the cultural capital that the Confucian tradition can contribute to the new century and millennium.

Plate 2 *An acolyte or guardian on a terrace in the Forest of Confucius. Such broad open spaces would have been the settings for Confucian lectures and debates.* Photo: Evelyn Berthrong.

2 THE CULTIVATION OF THE SELF

BEGINNING WITH BECOMING A PERSON: SELF-CULTIVATION

There is always a rhythm, style, and direction to Confucian life. The Confucian Way has a goal for the human maturation process. Moreover, from the Confucian viewpoint, the process or path to the goal, what is called the Dao, is inextricably linked to the goal. Goal and path are one process and cannot be understood in isolation from each other. In order to understand the goal, one must understand the path of Dao. A typical Western way to try to understand Confucianism would be to define the goal of the tradition, but from within the Confucian world, an equally valid method would be to ask, what is the process and how do we achieve it? It has been said that whereas a Western scholar will ask what something is, a Chinese scholar will ask, how do we accomplish the task and how is this task related to other similar tasks?

According to Confucius, the Dao was something as close as the palm of the hand. Moreover, he taught, "It is the person that is able to broaden the way (*dao*), not the way that broadens the person" (Ames and Rosemont, 1998, p.190; 15: 29). The Master Confucius would never let anyone forget that they were responsible for their own conduct. In fact, one of the best ways to understand the Confucian project is to think of it as the steadfast quest to become fully human. Again, the Master himself described the stages of the Confucian life as a series of steps toward the Way itself.

> From fifteen, my mind-heart was set upon learning;
> From thirty I took my stance;

From forty I was no longer doubtful;
From fifty I realized the propensities of *tian* (*tianming*);
From sixty my ear was attuned;
From seventy I could give my mind-heart free rein without overstepping
  the boundaries. (Ames and Rosemont, 1998, pp.76–77; 2:4)

The trick was to figure out what to learn along the way and then how to put that insight into service for oneself and others. Once the stance was found, then the rest would come through continued self-cultivation and education. At the end one could roam free without worrying about offending *tian* or other people. His disciples once recorded this conversation about the Master's teaching.

> "The Master said, 'Zeng, my friend! My Way is bound together with one continuous strand.' Master Zeng replied, 'Indeed.' When the Master had left, the disciples asked, 'What was he referring to?' Master Zeng said, 'The way of the Master is doing one's utmost (*zhong*) and putting oneself in the other's place (*shu*), nothing more.' (Ames and Rosemont, 1998, p.92; 4:15)

Of course, everyone realized that the Master was speaking of true humanity, the virtue of *ren*. Only a person of true humaneness could show the empathy and utmost courage to become a worthy person.

The great contemporary New Confucian, Mou Zongsan (1909–95), defined this primordial Confucian ethical sensibility as rooted in "concern consciousness." Mou believed that Greek philosophy's root metaphor was analysis and wonder about the nature of being. This is why those touched by Greek thought always ask the question of why something is as it is. Likewise, the great religions of Christianity, Judaism, Islam, and Hinduism have a metaphor of awe before the divine reality as the root of their spiritual experience. The characteristic mode of their experience is piety before the awesome character of the divine reality. Confucianism's root metaphor was and is a concern for the world. If we need to search for a Western analogy, the Quaker tradition surely provides one. Quakers speak of having a concern for the world; Confucians were taught that the Master's "one thread" was a constant and vigilant concern for self, family, community, society, nation, the world, and the beyond, the veritable Dao of all that was, is, and can be.

If one asks, where does this "concern consciousness" arise, the Confucian tradition always begins with the person as a social being. Of course, the primal aspect of human social being is the family. Confucians have been accused of idealizing the family. This is especially true after the rise of depth psychology, a modern Western medical therapy that has discovered that many people are damaged because of trauma within the family. Confucius knew all of this. He knew that blind reverence for the family values of filial piety and respect for the elders could be a mistake. In a passage that some Confucians found hard to understand, the Master mocks an old man. What could be more out of kilter with the stereotype of rigid Confucian morality that demanded respect for family and the elders? But it is clear that Confucius meant just what he said. There is nothing intrinsically good about an aged person who is without virtue. Likewise, there would be something wrong with a young person who did not respect a worthy elder. But concern for each person demands a reciprocity that flows both ways. An adult who is merely chronologically old does not merit reverence from the young. This is a hard teaching, but it fits with Confucius' persistent demand that we cultivate the way of virtue, and that this way is long and arduous.

Nonetheless, as countless generations of Confucian teachers have pointed out, for better or worse, we begin and are formed as human beings in our families. Xunzi, the third of the classical masters (after Confucius and Mencius), argued that human beings are unique because of their culture, i.e., the use of language and the ability to transmit cultural distinctions from generation to generation. He did not mean that human beings were separate from nature. Quite the contrary. Human beings were part of nature but with the added dimension of culture, and culture was the gift of language. Human beings had the chance to embody the full range of virtues according to Xunzi because we are social animals. We become full human beings, fully ethical persons within the larger human family. Thus, we all begin this journey, for better or worse, within the family. It is here that we practice language and learn about our traditions. Confucians emphasized the role of the family because they are "social" or relational philosophers. We become human in community; and community is worthy of being called civilized if and only if it is an ethical community of concern, reciprocity, and humaneness.

Confucianism, according to feminist analysis, is hopelessly authoritarian and perhaps even tyrannical because it is modeled on The Strict Father (to borrow a term from the modern linguist, George Lakoff). New Confucians, including feminist theorists, counter that while too many Confucians followed The Strict Father to very negative ends, we should not forget that the tradition also had The Nurturing Parent (also from Lakoff) as a model. To prove their point about The Nurturing Parent they can quote Mencius' condemnation of tyrants and the right of the people to revolt when suasion and reform fail, as well as the great lyrical Western Inscription of Zhang Zai (1020–77). In the Western Inscription Zhang praises the feelings of empathy, love, and concern that obtain within the family and argues that these need to be extended to embrace the whole cosmos.

Perhaps every great philosophy and religion is prone to a particular deformation specific to its root metaphor. Critics maintain that Confucianism, driven by its concern to be involved in the ordering of society, was too easily seduced into the service of less than worthy rulers. It is true that Confucians, for the most part, always believed that they had the obligation to serve the state as worthy and just ministers and civil servants. Of course, rulers knew this and would appeal to this Confucian sense of duty to overcome other scruples about how the ruler actually governed. There was a dance between the imperial government and the Confucian scholar. The problem is that the Confucians were prone to compromise with the authoritarian elements of statecraft. Confucian men also were more than willing to transfer the authoritarian aspects of imperial rule to family life. This last custom caused tragedy for the Confucian family, a social institution that should have been infused with affection, respect, deference, love, and compassion. Modern Confucians now argue that one of the main areas of self-cultivation must be the reform of the relationships between men and women towards a more just model.

From the beginning of the tradition, there has always been a debate as to whether the Confucian Way is a religion or a philosophy, or just a subtle form of social ethics. This argument makes sense because Confucians do have a complicated vision of the matrix of human culture and the responsibility of each person to cultivate her- or himself. In fact, Confucianism has been a combination of spiritual discernment, philosophic speculation, and social interaction. It depends on one's angle of approach. If the Way is considered social ethics, then it surely is with its teachings of humanity, reciprocity, and empathy. Moreover, these ethical virtues find their place in a civilized society. If one spends time thinking about *tian* or heaven, then one might well embrace a religious dimension of the Confucian Way. One will ask ultimate questions about how a person can conform to the mandate of heaven, the famous notion of *tianming.* Whoever asks about learning and the history of the tradition will philosophize in a Confucian mode. Study and reflection on the great classical texts will cause one to wonder how they are to be understood and applied to the conduct of daily life.

There are vertical and horizontal dimensions that bind Confucian life into a unified, coherent Way. The vertical dimension is the desire to cultivate the self in order to put oneself in tune with the Way. This is what Confucius meant when he talked about giving the mind-heart a free rein, to be in touch or conformed to the Dao as the Way of heaven. But there is also the need to cultivate harmonious and respectful relations with other people. This is the horizontal dimension of Confucian life. Confucians never make the case that their tradition is grounded in the mundane details of the world. There is no room for Confucian action outside of the world. When pressed on this point once, Confucius replied that if he could not live with other human beings, where could he live? But mere biological survival is not what is meant. To live a civilized life is the goal; the method is self-cultivation; the hope is to become an authentic person who embodies the virtue of humaneness in all dimensions of human life.

A Confucian scholar such as Dr. Li would employ a number of methods to achieve the ultimate goals of Confucian life. Because the Confucian tradition always focuses on the middle range of human life, it is not hard to understand why these goals would be specified in ethical terms. Ethics define how we live our lives together. The goal of Confucian life, as we shall see, is to create a peaceful world. In order to create such a world, we need ethical norms. Furthermore, the Confucians were convinced that we needed to expend a great deal of effort in cultivating these ethical norms that would ultimately allow us to take part in civilized human society. One of the starting points of the Confucian Way was the elaboration of many forms of self-cultivation. It was the conviction of generations of Confucians that descriptions of various forms of self-cultivation were provided by the sages and worthies to assist the person to achieve full humanity as defined in ultimately ethical terms.

The ultimate goal of Confucian self-cultivation was to become a sage, the highest achievement within the Confucian world of thought and practice. Sages were rare, but they did exist, and it was the task of all sincere Confucians to try to match themselves to the virtues of the sage. Theoretically any person could become a sage. The powers of a true sage were awesome. As the *Doctrine of the Mean* taught, the perfected sage could form a triad with heaven and earth. The Confucian tradition understood this teaching to mean that the sage tapped into the vital force or spirit of creativity itself. In fact, the cosmos could only be completed or perfected if and when the sage played his or her part in the unceasing generativity of the Dao. It was no wonder that the later Neo-Confucians such as Zhu Xi (1130–1200) considered this the most sublime teaching to be found in any of the classics. However, as the great Western philosopher Spinoza noted, everything rare and wonderful is also exceedingly difficult to realize.

Although there could be many different ways to cultivate the self, two of the most respected and elaborated forms were study and reflection and a distinct Confucian form of meditation, often called honoring human nature. The selection of these two forms of self-cultivation were pragmatic and reached a fulsome culmination in the Song dynasty renewal of the Confucian Way. However, it is crucial to remember that the Song model was based on the previous generations of Confucian experiments in realizing the Way as the manifestation of what human life ought to become. The experience of generations of Confucian scholars confirmed that the methods worked – that study and meditation were techniques, when rightly applied, that could help the scholar become an ethical person.

Another distinct form of Confucian meditation was called quiet-sitting. It became a staple of Confucian self-cultivation in the Song dynasty and remained a feature of the Confucian Way down to the modern period. It is a fascinating feature of Confucian life because it shows how the tradition developed over time. Quiet-sitting was not, like study as a form of self-cultivation, a feature of early Confucian life. The success of quiet-sitting, when it was formalized in the middle period of Confucian history (1000–1644), demonstrates that the story of Confucianism is one of growth and chance. Too often Confucianism is likened to a frozen fossil; nothing could be farther from the truth.

For instance, the classical warrant for the practice of quiet-sitting was found in one of the canonical texts of the Confucian tradition. This was the famous teaching in the *Great Learning* that described the generation of a just and harmonious society based on self-cultivation. The description of the process was read in two directions. The ultimate goal for society was the creation of peace through the entire world. The way to do this was expressed in the admonition that "from the Son of Heaven down to the common people, all must regard cultivation of the personal life as the root or foundation" (Chan, 1963, p.87).

Confucian life was a commitment to becoming fully human, to realizing all the worthy human nature endowed in each person by heaven.
According to the Confucian tradition, a person had an obligation to cultivate the self in order to be of service to oneself and to others. The goal
for both self-cultivation and service to others was the creation of a peaceful world. The vision was predicated on the assumption that the task of
becoming fully and authentically human could only be accomplished
within a social setting. A person was formed first in the family, the local
community, through education, and then in service to the broader world
of local, regional, and national service. All of these interlocking levels
depended on each other for positive reinforcement. As the tradition
taught, this process of self-cultivation leading to full humanity was a
long and arduous one. Nonetheless, it was not a joyless search. Its ultimate goal was peace defined as a harmonious and rich human life for all
peoples. From the Confucian point of view, the road was long but the
ultimate destination was worth the effort. The task was to discover the
most appropriate means to follow the path. Confucians, from time
immemorial, depended on the joint support of self-cultivation and education in order to reach these goals. They were nurtured in their project
by the affection and support of the family and by the generalized civility
of society that they called ritual action.

The process of self-cultivation was also described as a broadening
and a deepening of the human person. The broadening depends on the
fact that a human being only becomes fully human in relationship to
other persons. We all begin life in a family and then move out toward
increasingly complex social relationships. These relationships help define
who we are. From the viewpoint of the Confucian scholar, all of these
human relationships have an ethical character to them. Human growth
is a broadening of vision, of relationship, and of the ethical bonds that
hold people together in community from the intimate confines of the
family to the vast expanse of the Chinese empire and beyond.

The deepening process comes with reflection on the ethical dimensions of broadening through social interactions. A person thus realizes
that there is a vertical dimension as well as a horizontal dimension to life.
The horizontal connects us to other people and to society, whereas the
vertical connects us to the Dao itself. The whole process can be described
as a journey that moves through six major stages. The first stage is the
cultivation of the self. The second focuses on the life of the family. The
third moves from the family out to the larger community. The fourth

stage expands this social concern toward the country. The fifth stage moves from the country to the whole world. The sixth stage moves beyond even the world of human beings, the countries beyond China, onwards to a concern for the cosmos. Some of the great Song philosophers argued that the worthy person was as in tune with the grass outside of a scholar's study as focused on the affairs of the empire or the affection found in a stable family life. What is crucial is to see all the six stages as mutually depending on each other for support.

One helpful image is to conceive of the self-cultivation project as the alternation between field and focus. The field metaphor addresses the location of a person at any point in their life. A young person will be "focused" on the field of the family. Later in life, the focus will be broader. However, more exposure to the world will also make the focus deeper and richer over time. The person is a focus in a field that is constantly growing. Growth characterizes the whole process. The very first of the classical texts, the *Book of Changes*, taught that Dao was ceaseless generativity.

The metaphor of field and focus is linked to the earlier observation of the difference between the what-questions of Western thought and the how-questions of Confucian philosophy. The what-question seeks for a crisp definition of what it means to be fully human in the Confucian tradition. However, the Confucian thinker does not approach the question in this fashion, or at least not all the time. What is more likely is to seek a balance between the particular focus of the self and the dynamic action of the larger field, often call the Dao or Way. There is a feeling of movement from focus to field and field back to focus that keeps the whole reflection focused on the process rather than any particular moment. The how-question is flexible because it does not expect to uncover some unchanging core to reality. Rather, the basic issue is to find a way to be civilized amid the changing patterns of personal maturation and social interaction.

In order to provide a curriculum for such self-cultivation, the Southern Song master Zhu Xi selected four classical works to provide a ladder into the complicated world of Confucian texts for beginning students. The idea was that the Confucian canon was so large that it was impossible to find a good place to focus without some special texts to provide an initial insight into the patterns of the whole field of Confucian culture. These four texts were known as the *Four Books* – The *Analects* of Confucius, the *Mencius*, the *Great Learning*, and the *Doctrine of the*

Mean – and they became the canon within a canon for Confucians ever since the Song dynasty. All aspiring Confucian scholars had to master these four texts. Yet, for the true Confucian, the mere verbal mastery of the text was not the point of the exercise. The real point was to help society achieve peace and harmony. The texts were ways, when really understood and embodied in life, into Confucian culture.

However, things were not really made as simple as they might sound by having a beginning point of only four texts. Just because students began at one point did not mean that there was complete agreement on how self-cultivation should be accomplished. There were endless debates among Confucian scholars about what Confucius meant and how Confucius wanted students to proceed in the study of the Way. One of the key debates focused on the description of how to begin the whole course of study. The text taught that in order to bring peace to the world, a person must begin by rectifying the mind-heart. And in order to rectify their mind-hearts, people must rectify or make their will sincere. The last step in the process was specified in the *Doctrine of the Mean* as "those who wish to make their wills sincere would first extend their knowledge. The extension of knowledge consists in the investigation of things" (Chan, 1963, p.86).

The Confucian tradition was flexible in providing ways to follow the true Way. Confucius was famous for being a skilled teacher: he devised different methods of instruction for each student, methods specifically suited to the gifts of the particular person. Whereas the methods for self-cultivation might vary, the ultimate goal, of becoming a full person within a peaceful society, never varied. Confucius called the prime virtue of self-cultivation *ren* or humaneness. It was the pursuit of this goal via the cultivation of humaneness that made the Confucian quest endlessly rewarding.

QUIET-SITTING

Master Zhu once wrote that a Confucian should spend half a day studying and half a day in quiet-sitting. By this he meant to include both self-cultivation via quiet-sitting and education through study of the Confucian classics. Zhu was often criticized for encouraging a meditation practice closer to Daoism and Buddhism than to classical Confucianism. The critics went on to point out that Confucius himself argues that it was better to study than waste time in meditation. Master Zhu countered by noting that there had to be some method to "make the will sincere." For many students, a mixture of quiet-sitting meditation and study was the ideal form of self-cultivation. Whatever might have been the most ancient forms of Confucian education and self-cultivation, by the Song dynasty quiet-sitting had become an accepted part of the Confucian Way.

The name quiet-sitting came from the characteristic technique of Confucian meditation. Rather than assuming a lotus position on the floor, as would be the norm for Buddhist meditation, the Confucian sat in a chair. With back straight, eyes slightly down, and with the hands on the knees, the Confucian began the process of cultivating the mind-heart. The aim of Confucian quiet-sitting was to let the mind-heart become still, to dwell in a quiet mode so that the mind-heart could be examined in terms of its fundamental human nature. There is an old metaphor that says the mind-heart is like a monkey, constantly running around its mental world. While at one level the liveliness of the mind-heart is praiseworthy, at other times it poses a problem for Confucian self-cultivation. Quiet-sitting is the way to achieve these states of contemplative calm with the mind-heart focused carefully, listening to itself, and remaining still and calm. Moreover, the *Doctrine of the Mean* taught that within the mind-heart there was a quiet state of centrality before engagement with the world; if one could realize this balance, then a person could respond with harmony to the external reality of the quotidian life.

However, for the Confucian, the goal of quiet-sitting is not just to achieve a quiet mind-heart. Confucians were critical of Daoists and Buddhists for mistaking the real aim of meditation: it was to perfect and cultivate the mind-heart and not to remain in some kind of quasi-independent mental state. Remembering Confucius' dictum, if quiet-sitting did not help understanding, then it was useless. And if understanding did not lead to ethical action, then it was not really understanding as the great Ming dynasty reformer Wang Yangming (1472–1529) so forcefully taught. There must be a unity of theory and action, of ethics and contemplation. Wang explained that this was the act of extending good will (*zhi liangzhi*) as he put it in his famous formula for cultivating the mind-heart

Of course, all Confucians knew that a life without the active search for *ren* or humaneness was not a Confucian life. Humaneness was the ultimate goal, however difficult or elusive it was to achieve. Confucius' own model was crucial here. Although Confucius never claimed to achieve humaneness, he never wavered from trying to seek it either.

Some great Ming dynasty Confucian teachers even developed ways of examining the conscience each day as a way to seek humaneness. They would write in a journal about whether or not they had followed the path of humanity and justice during the day. These explorations of the human conscience followed the ledgers of merit and demerit that Chinese popular religious teachers proposed for their students. At the simplest level, the student was urged to write down a list of the positive and negative things they had thought and done during the day. It was not enough merely not to record that something bad had happened. It was also crucial to look long and hard at the mind-heart and see if there were evil or uncivil thoughts lurking deep in the mind-heart. Liu Zongzhou (d. 1645), the last of the great Ming masters, adopted the phrase "vigilance in solitude" to describe this exercise.

Dr. Li focused his reflections on whether or not he came close to humaneness during the day. This was an exercise in humility. In order to check on his progress in very specific and concrete terms, the next step was to think about *xiao* or filial piety.

Confucians believed that ethical life must begin with the family; and family life was built upon filial piety. This was a way to bring the focus of self-cultivation away from the person's mind-heart outward to the wider world, but not too wide to begin with. Again, there was a distinction in the Confucian worldview between the socially engaged quest for ethical action and the Daoist and Buddhist proclivities toward excessive quietism.

From the Confucian point of view, there always had to be a balance between the inner and outer dimensions of human life. The very beginning of the outer life was filial piety. The third step was to move beyond filial piety and the family into the broader world. When Confucius was once asked what he would do to reform the state, he answered that he would rectify terms. This seemed a bit odd to the interrogator, and Confucius went on to make the point that only in a really well ordered state could you make the case that names and reality were in unison. For instance, only in an ethically functioning family could a father and son relate to each other in a correct fashion. The analogy held for the state. Only in a proper or just state could a minister serve the ruler and could the ruler be said to hold the mandate of heaven. The key term here was *zheng*, or to correct or make correct. The semantic range carried the meanings of proper, formal, to correct, straightforward, unbiased or sharp.

The aim of the exercise was to allow the mind-heart to move from the reflections on humaneness to filial conduct outwards toward proper conduct in the wider world of society and the state. Of course, all three elements were inseparable. All were necessary to claim the Confucian life. By stilling the mind-heart in quiet-sitting a person could take stock of their life and see where more effort was needed, more insight required, and more study appropriate.

Of course, this was only one possible variation of quiet-sitting. Here the Buddhist concept of *upāya* (skillful means) was helpful. Each person was different so a meditation teacher needed to specify a different path for each student. The timid needed to be made bold and the reckless needed to be restrained. Long ago Confucius was asked why he has given such different instructions to his students faced with similar tasks. Confucius, in seeking to help each student find the Way, gave them teachings appropriate to the task and to their personal characteristics. As with so much else in Confucian life, the ultimate goal was a balance between the various levels and dimensions of human conduct. The main thing in quiet-sitting was to still the mind-heart enough to be able to ponder the spiritual dimensions of mundane life. Although no Confucian sought escape from the world, the rectification of the world needed a calm and reflective mind-heart. It was the question of finding the balance point between the inner and outer life that was crucial for self-cultivation. While the goal of balance was clear, the way to achieve it was difficult, and the difficulty was more than just psychological or even spiritual.

Dr. Li believed the problem could only be solved by reconciling the two major methods of cultivation as taught by Zhu Xi and Wang Yangming. Simplistic though it might seem, the two necessary moments were the "examination of thing" or *gewu* and "extending the good will" or *zhi liangzhi*. Both admonitions summarized the Confucian quest for a balanced form of self-cultivation. Yet there was a creative tension between the two.

Briefly, the examination of things was the counsel to take the world seriously as a source of study. Confucians prided themselves as having what they called a solid or realistic teaching that they compared and contrasted to Taoist and Buddhist philosophy. From the Confucian viewpoint, Taoists and Buddhists taught doctrines characterized by the Buddhist theory of the emptiness of all phenomenal reality and the Taoist teaching of nothingness, that the source of all being was nothingness. Confucians proudly reversed this order and argued that the world was real and pluralistic. Therefore, in order to understand reality, a student must attend to the world in all its problematic glory. The method Master Zhu emphasized, based on the *Great Learning*, was the practice of "examining things."

Of course, Master Zhu did not mean that all we had to do was wander around looking at a sunset or smelling the flowers. The phrase "examining things" had a much deeper meaning for him. We examine things in order to discover their ultimate principles and meanings (see Chapter 4, Transmitting the Dao, for details). Furthermore, what Master Zhu meant by "things" was expansive and not narrowly focused on the material things of the world, though it certainly included these as well. Master Zhu was a keen observer of the natural world as well as human nature and history. For instance, he was one of the first scholars to recognize the meaning of fossils. Although he was clearly fascinated by these strange animals cast in rock, he sought to understand what this ancient tale tells us about the world. The conclusion that Master Zhu drew from the discovery of the fossils was the great age and ceaseless transformation of the cosmos. This was the lesson or principle found in the investigation of this natural phenomenon.

Master Zhu also talked about things and what he called *shi* or what might be termed events in some cases. For instance, he was more interested in patterns of ethical conduct than in fossils per se, if the truth be told. For him, a decent ethical action, carried out with ritual aplomb, was just as real as the fossil in the rock. We must remember that for all the Confucians the payoff to any action whatsoever was its ethical value or weight in the social order. Later scholars often remarked that what Master Zhu most emphasized in his teaching of the examination of things was the study of texts. In short, what Zhu was really getting at was a hermeneutic art of reading the world in order to understand our place in it. The most important "things and events" that we would uncover in the process were ethical patterns or norms. The world was shot through and through with values according to Zhu, and it was our duty to cultivate our minds so that we are in tune with the patterns of virtuous order and so that we will act on what we have learned.

Wang Yangming really did not disagree with Master Zhu about the need to cultivate virtuous conduct, to sustain a good will in all our interactions with people and indeed the whole world. The argument was about method and the proper place to begin the process of self-cultivation. Wang's major worry was that Master Zhu's method, although it might work for some students, was prone to one potentially fatal flaw. The flaw was the possibility of the fragmentation of effort and focus. Wang was worried that the student would be drawn into the external world and would become lost among the beauties and frivolities of the mundane life. Of course, Wang, like Zhu, affirmed that we can only situate ourselves in this mundane world. There is no other world or realm of emptiness or nothingness as the Daoists and Buddhists suggested.

The problem was not the multifarious plenitude of the world per se. At one point when he was very young, Wang Yangming had tried, along with a group of friends, to follow Master Zhu's admonition to examine things by sitting in front of a bamboo grove in order to discover the principle of bamboo. Although Wang managed to sit longer than all of his friends, he eventually confessed to his failure to understand the real nature of the bamboo any better after his examination of them than before he began.

It was only later that Wang Yangming realized that his failure with the bamboo resided in the method. As he had experimented with examining the bamboo in the garden he had lost himself in the external world. He had failed to realize that he needed to attend to his own will or inclination to study. Until and unless he was able to focus his will on the task of self-cultivation, then he would fail no matter how much he read texts or studied the natural world around him. Without good will he would have no focused way to make sense of anything in the external world. It was like saying that you were a filial son and yet acted disrespectfully to your father and mother. This was not real learning; it was merely knowing a few verbal phrases drawn from the classics. Real knowledge, Wang taught, could only be found in the conjunction of discernment and action: if you claimed to be filial, this was only a reality if you were actually and fully dedicated to the well-being of your parents in thought, action, and word.

Wang, along with generations of Confucian scholars, marked this distinction in cultivation with the tags of "honoring the nature" or the "path of query and study." These were two phrases taken from the *Doctrine of the Mean* and they were used to indicate which starting point was to be used by the student. Those who followed the way of honoring the nature would follow Master Wang and his emphasis on making the will sincere. Only with a sincere will focused on a reverence for the Way of the sages and worthies could the student make progress in self-cultivation. Those who embraced the path of query and study emphasized the need to attend to the reading of texts and the examination of the world in all its natural and social glory.

Actually, all the great Confucian teachers agreed that the honoring of the nature and the path of query and study could not be separated. The hermeneutic circle was linked. Some perhaps needed more reflection on the will and others needed the discipline of textual study. Dr. Li preferred to combine both methods in his own quiet-sitting.

Following another common self-cultivation practice, Dr. Li consulted a small book that he kept in his study. It was like a diary and in fact each day he did write a short entry. The entries were, however, of a specific nature, and were often of two different kinds. Typically he would record when he had success in his ethical or emotional life or when he failed on either count. As the classics taught, the most difficult part of the practice was with the human will and intentions. It was easy for anyone to look the part of a virtuous person. But if that is all that you did, the Confucian tradition taught that you were then merely a thief of virtue. You stole the name of virtue without the true substance.

The more difficult task was not only to do the good but likewise will the good, and to do all of this for the right reasons. For instance, if what pleased you and ritual coincided, then there was little merit in your action. However, if what was demanded was odious to you and you still did it, even if no one would have noticed what you did, then this was an improvement. The real trick was to be able to see that even though you did not want to do whatever you were supposed to do and yet cultivate the calm reflection that it was your duty, then you had made progress.

Dr. Li decided to meditate on filial piety and family responsibilities. The beginning of the session was simple. You sat in your favorite chair with your hands calmly placed on your knees. The basic posture of Confucian quiet-sitting was just what it sounded like. In this regard it was different from most Buddhist meditation forms that had you sit on the floor in a lotus posture.

After settling into the chair, you would keep your back as straight as possible. You wanted good posture, but posture was not the aim actually. Good posture helped you be alert and not focus too much attention on the state of your body's position. Then you began the process of quieting the mind-heart. In the Chinese tradition the mind-heart was likened to a monkey. It was one of the trio of the horse of the will and the pig of the appetites. The metaphoric names indicated what Chinese culture thought was the particular problem with each of these parts of human motivation.

The monkey mind-heart was the most difficult to cope with because it would dart around the mental and memory world of the person trying to meditate. If there was a sound from outside the study, it would take the opportunity of chasing after the sound, and then thinking about the sound, and then thinking about something else. Before the person knew it, the monkey mind-heart was ten thousand miles from the task at hand. Or even when the mind began to calm itself, some worry or concern could arise and distract the mind-heart from letting go of all the verbal and emotional clutter of daily life.

Once the mind-heart began to clear, to become calm, then you had to decide what to concentrate on for the session. Sometimes it was a phrase or even an image. Sometimes all you tried to do was to get the mind-heart to rest in silence. For this session Dr. Li had selected to think about filial piety in the context of his family life. The particular object of his attention was the upcoming marriage of his wife's niece. His wife was very fond of the niece and was playing a major role in the preparations for the wedding.

Normally this would not have caused any problems whatsoever, but the preparations for the wedding and the wedding itself were taking place in the busiest time of year for the magistrate. Moreover, there was even a special review of his work by the local censor (an examining official in charge of checking on the work of other officials). Nothing seemed to warrant any serious worry, but Dr. Li's attention was fixed on making sure that everything went as smoothly as possible in preparation for the reports and review. The problem he faced was the tension between his personal life and his public responsibilities.

Of course, his main duty was to his office and the care of the people under his administration. However, the Confucian tradition also demanded concern for his family as well. How did he reconcile to the two competing duties? The first thing was to let the mind-heart become calm enough that he could review his emotional state and question the state of his will to find out why he was disturbed. What he was most concerned about was the fact that he was worried about the wedding interfering with his official duties. This was a problem of letting his emotions interfere with his official life, which, of course, as a magistrate, could not be separated from the rest of his world.

Dr. Li found his monkey mind-heart playing a typical trick. It raced off and asked: Why are you worrying about this silly problem anyway? There is nothing really that important in all of this. It is a minor problem. This was an all too easy way to answer the question. After stilling the mind-heart by letting go of this thought gently, Dr. Li concentrated on his breathing for a moment. One of the best ways to practice quiet-sitting was to become aware of your breath going out and coming in. It was a calming procedure that allowed for a more balanced mental state.

As he meditated on the problem at hand, Dr. Li took solace in the fact that the Master had taught that to be worthy of major things you also had to be in calm control of minor daily events as well. One needed to be filial and responsible to official duty. This was not the direction in which the meditation should flow if there was to be progress. Rather, in the stillness of the study, Dr. Li realized what he needed to do.

He needed to begin at the beginning. And the beginning of filial piety, as with so many other Confucian virtues, rested in a careful weighing of the duties of reciprocity. Reciprocity itself could only be efficacious and living, rather than just some mechanical formula, if it was defined by empathy. It was the empathy that was missing in the analysis and his feelings and will. Of course, you cannot force the human will to be empathetic. To be empathetic demands a quality of ethical calmness that takes the time to try to see why the other person is acting or feeling as they are. As a magistrate, Dr. Li knew this so well; without empathy you could do very little for people. Confucius had taught that you should treat those below you in status as you would like to be treated by those above you, and you should, likewise, treat those above you just like you would like your subordinates to treat you. The duties and obligations might be different for each station in life. For instance, as a father you needed to keep your young son from falling into a well even if the young boy was curious about looking into the mouth of the well.

BACK TO THE WORLD

One thing should be made very clear about the majority of Confucians' understanding of quiet-sitting. It was never to be an end in and of itself. Wang Yangming, as well as being a truly great philosopher, was also a successful general and poet. There was nothing otherworldly or unconnected about Wang when he arose from meditation. In fact, meditation was a tool for sharpening the mind-heart. Further, the sharpness, the discernment of the mind-heart was of a special kind. It was, first, the ability to see things clearly. In this there was nothing different in quiet-sitting to differentiate the method from Buddhist and Daoist forms of meditation.

But second, Confucian quiet-sitting was a sharpening of the mind-heart into an ethical awareness of the way things are. The Confucian went forth from quiet-sitting with a reverent, sincere mind-heart that had the ability to see and act in a proper way. The ultimate end, as Wang Yangming had taught incessantly, was to fuse knowledge and action into a seamless web of proper and timely behavior. Quiet-sitting was judged useless until and unless it helped to bring about just and harmonious action.

The particular genius of quiet-sitting was the recognition that in order for human beings to see truly we must often calm the mind-heart. A mind-heart overwhelmed with confused, obscure, or conflicting thoughts and emotions is going to have a terrible time dealing with the world in any coherent, ethical fashion. While quiescence is not a goal sufficient unto itself, it is an important step for most people. In this sense, Confucian quiet-sitting was resolutely pragmatic. Although the results of quiet-sitting were often pleasant and refreshing, they were considered insufficient without recourse to ethical and socially useful action. Simply to reside in quiescence, to think and feel nothing, was to become like a piece of dead wood, Master Zhu taught. A piece of dead wood might be useful for building a fire, but the actual fire of life demanded an empathetic consciousness that was embodied in and prepared to be energetically and even passionately engaged in the struggle for justice and righteous social and personal conduct. Quiet-sitting was understood to be a way to achieve these humane ends.

Plate 3 *A modern rendering of the young Mencius and his mother installed in the middle of a busy traffic circle in Zòu. Mencius' mother was a famed as a model for women who teach their children.* Photo: Evelyn Berthrong.

3 EDUCATING THE PERSON

THE IMPORTANCE OF EDUCATION

Education plays a crucial role in the Confucian Way for two major reasons. The first is pragmatic. One of the things Confucians have been most proud of over the centuries is the openness of their vision of society. Of course, Confucians are not modern egalitarian democrats and always have had a highly refined sense of decorum, deference, and hierarchy. However, from the Han dynasty to the very end of the imperial era in 1911, Confucians argued for "careers open to talent." Confucians believed that if a ruler wanted to be successful he needed to recruit and listen to his ministers. Although Confucians believed deeply in families, they also understood that a brilliant father did not always produce brilliant children.

One of the main questions for Confucian thinkers was how to find a way to recruit and staff the civil service needed to run a huge empire. We need to remember that China is the longest successful human experience in state formation. After the unification of the empire by the Qin and Han in the third century B.C.E., the empire prevailed for more than two thousand years. Of course, there were periods of disunion, but they were always viewed as dangerous and distasteful. The dream, which often became reality, was always of a unified empire. Dynastic names such as Han, Tang, Song, Ming, and Qing speak of the glories of Chinese culture and state formation. It was a vast world, as large as or even larger than the Roman empire. The only empires that held more territory were the great Mongol empires of the twelfth to fourteenth centuries and the modern Russian empire (which was followed by the Soviet Union until 1989). Some people have argued that the only two great empires left in the world are the Chinese and the American. Obviously, the Chinese empire is much, much older.

The importance of education in Confucianism is not surprising at all when we remember that one of the favorite titles for Confucius was the "First Teacher." He was also known as the "Teacher of the Ten Thousand Generations." Moreover, Confucius was justly famous for being the first private teacher in China. Of course, there had been schools and teachers before Confucius, but they had always been connected with the government of the various states of their time. Each state had a school for the sons of the nobles; it was from these schools that officials for the various offices of the states were recruited. What was most important was birth.

Confucius was renowned for being willing to teach anyone who wanted to learn. In fact, he was only interested in students who burned to learn about the Zhou culture he revered as the source of civilized life. He believed that his mission in life was to restore the early culture of the founders of the Zhou dynasty. Kings Wen and Wu and the Duke of Zhou were his culture heroes. Confucius was convinced that if he could revive the glories of early Zhou culture through education then there would be a general revival of civilized social life for all the people of the Middle Kingdom.

What was also amazing for the time was that many of Confucius' students were from the ranks of commoners. He was firmly convinced that it was moral and intellectual ability that was important rather than birth. He did not turn away young aristocrats who sought him out as a teacher, but he was equally committed to his less noble followers as well. In terms of recommending his students it was their talent and not their social rank or noble birth that caused him to commend them to the rulers of the day.

According to scholars of ancient and classical China (c. 1200 B.C.E. to c. 200 C.E.), Confucius was born into the lowest stratum of aristocratic society. He was a *shi* or what is often translated as a knight in English. Confucius lost his father very early and was raised by his mother. He clearly received a fine classical education, though he himself confessed that he had learned all sorts of other things because of the humble circumstances of his family. He went on to a career of service in minor posts in his native state of Lu. As the story is told, frustrated that his ruler would not listen to his advice, he set out upon his way to search for old records of the early sage kings. It was during these travels between the various states that he collected a group of students and disciples.

In a nutshell, Confucius argued that there was a crisis in the China of his time. The formerly great Zhou dynasty had fallen on hard times; the various other feudal states no longer allowed Zhou to rule or to reign. Confucius had a simple solution for this grave political and social crisis. All that was needed was to restore the Chinese world to the glory of the early Zhou kings and the Duke of Zhou. Confucius believed that such a revival was possible. There were enough writings left for a serious student of morality to understand the culture of the Zhou founders and other sage kings of antiquity.

Confucius continued the plot by purportedly collecting the basic texts into what later generations of scholars call the Confucian classics. In Confucius' day the classics numbered five. By the Song dynasty (960–1279), the number was raised to thirteen as some of the older texts were split into separate works and other important early writings were added. From the Confucian viewpoint, the growth from five to thirteen only bespoke of an organizational increase and not the addition of texts written after Confucius' own time.

Of course, later scholars came to doubt that this was an entirely accurate story. Critical Chinese, Korean, and Japanese scholars realized that Confucius simply did not have a personal authorial or editorial hand in all the classics credited to him; moreover, some of the texts were clearly written as late as the early part of the Han dynasty (c. 100 B.C.E.). Most of the great classical canon was made up of texts put together layer by layer over time. Nonetheless, there was little doubt that Confucius was inspired by these classical texts and the images and stories of the early sages and worthies. He loved and taught what he believed to be the core of early Zhou culture.

No matter who wrote or edited what, without doubt the tradition Confucius passed on was highly textual. In many respects the Confucian Way resembles the great Rabbinical tradition in the history of Judaism. Just as Moses would have been startled to discover that he founded Judaism as a new religion, Confucius would have been nonplussed to discover that later Western scholars invented a new word, Confucianism, to describe the tradition he so revered. From Confucius' viewpoint, he was a transmitter and not a creator. However, in the transmission there was also transformation, which Confucius also knew very well indeed.

For instance, Confucius based his teachings on the wisdom of the

Zhou dynasty and not the earlier Shang and Xia dynasties. The reason
for his choice was partially pragmatic and partially idealistic. In the first
place, Confucius believed that he did not have sufficient access to the
records of the Shang and Xia dynasties. The only records that he felt
secure about were from the Zhou. Even though he knew that many Zhou
records had been lost over the centuries, the accumulated deposit of
Zhou culture was rich enough to be the basis of a curriculum. In the
second place, Confucius believed that the early Zhou rulers, because they
were sages and worthies, were able to carry on the essence of the culture
of the earlier dynasties in a refined way. Kings Wen and Wu and the
Duke of Zhou were able to survey the history of early sages and transmitted these teachings to later generations.

Moreover, modern scholars hold that Confucius, along with being a
shi, also belonged to the group called *ru*. The definition of *ru* is a hotly
contested issue. One of the earliest meanings was something like "weak-
lings." It did not seem like a very good title for the followers of the First
Teacher. Whatever the term originally meant, it seems to have designated
a whole class of ritual specialists. These were men who served as experts
in the complicated ritual life of early China from the village level to the
highest echelons of the courts of Zhou China. From the archaeological
and historical record we know that ritual theory and conduct was a
crucial aspect of Zhou culture. In fact, a cultured person had to know
the correct ritual for every situation. There obviously was a need for
ritual specialists to advise the rulers of Confucius' day.

Confucians were certainly all *ru* though it is not clear whether all
early *ru* were followers of Confucius. But over time the two categories
became closely identified. What was the glue that held the *ru* Confucians
together as a group? The first aspect of their teaching was, as we have
noted, a mastery of ritual practice and theory. The second aspect was a
mastery of the growing body of written works that explained the theory
and practice of ritual and other topics of interest to the ruling elite of
classical China.

The new written texts displayed the aura of authority in early China.
The people of East Asia have always revered the written and (later)
printed word. There are even ceremonies for the burning of old books.
The early Confucians realized this and used their texts to claim certain
kinds of authority. It was a subtle move. The ritual specialists began by
serving the rulers and then, slowly and perhaps even somewhat uncon-
sciously, turned the tables. The particular collection of recorded sayings

attributed to Confucius, the *Lunyu* or *Analects*, made this point conclusively.

What Confucius taught was that even the greatest ruler was subject to the mandate of heaven. According to the rhetoric of the early founders of the Zhou dynasty, the Shang rulers had lost the mandate of heaven to rule China, because they had become immoral tyrants. The people, led by the Zhou rulers, had the right, even the obligation, to set things right by overthrowing the former dynastic rulers. As Confucians ceaselessly reminded rulers over and over again, heaven hears as the people hear, heaven speaks as the people speak. The only thing that heaven wants to hear is good reports from the people about the ruler. The ruler's only claim to the mandate of heaven is a just, harmonious, and peaceful social order. When a ruler becomes unjust or tyrannical, then, as Mencius taught, the people have the right to replace the evil ruler with a new, good one. This was the famous Confucian right of revolt.

The Confucians, of course, offered the rulers something else besides a doctrine of rebellion. They offered their services to the court as long as the court maintained (theoretically) a decent level of official conduct. Thus commenced the long dance between the rulers and their Confucian officials. Each party needed the other. The rulers needed a culturally sophisticated elite to help them rule. The Confucians provided a cadre of potential officials who were neither military men nor members of the ruling elite, the two groups that much too often were prone to getting ideas of replacing the ruler. The Confucians maintained their sense of dignity with the theory that the ruler had the obligation to listen to their advice.

Some rulers actually did listen to their Confucian advisors. In the 130s B.C.E., the Han Emperor Wu made the Confucian texts the official orthodoxy. This orthodox status was sustained for the Confucian school and their texts till 1905 when the imperial examination system based on the Confucian teachings was finally abolished in favor of more modern, Western styles, of education. Yet for all these centuries the civil society of China was formed by the early teachings of the Zhou Confucian masters. It was their favorite texts that became the educational curriculum for the empire.

TEXTS AND COMMENTARIES

With the central role of texts as the basis for teaching and education, it was almost natural for the Confucian tradition to develop commentaries on their classics. There were two major reasons for commentaries to be written. First, there was the great destruction of books and records that followed upon the savage wars of unification that led to the formation of the first great Chinese empire, the Qin. Part of the legend of the Qin is that, upon the advice of distinctly anti-Confucian advisors, known as the Legalists, the first Qin emperor ordered the destruction of most books in the empire. Actually, the emperor kept copies of these banned texts for the imperial library, but that did not help very much when this grand library, and many others, were destroyed in the civil wars that followed the fall of the Qin dynasty.

When the Han rulers finally reunited the empire in 206 B.C.E., the textual situation was in chaos like everything else. The grand legacies of the Confucians, as well as the other schools of the Warring States era, were scattered to the winds – or fires, or floods or other forms of destruction. One of the first tasks for the early generations of the Han Confucians was to restore as much of the classical written heritage as they could. They collected, collated, and edited as much as possible from the carnage of the founding and fall of the Qin and the victory of the Han. All future Confucians owe a debt of immense gratitude to the Han scholars who saved what could be saved of the classical tradition.

After having collected the fragments of the lost and banned works, the Han scholars immediately went to work writing elaborate commentaries on their beloved texts. They did so in order to explicate the materials that they had collected and edited. For instance, in some cases they would explain why there were fewer chapters than had been reported before. The Han editors wrote that they reduced redundancies in the older text. The second reason to write commentaries was the need to explicate the meaning of the texts. Although the classics were all written in what is called classical or literary Chinese, that is to say, the formal written language developed even prior to the Zhou dynasty, this does not mean that the texts were always easy to understand in the Han period. There could be hundreds of years separating the initial compilation of a text and its redaction by the Han scholars. The text needed commentaries and the best Han Confucians provided copious emendations, notes, and explanations to the classical texts.

Why commentaries rather than new, original work? We must remember that the commentaries played multiple roles. First, they served to explain complicated or confusing points in the earlier texts. Second, they were a form of piety towards the collected wisdom of the sages.

Although the Confucian tradition did not posit a theory of revelation from heaven or the gods for their classics, they did venerate them as the recorded words and deeds of the great sage kings and worthy ministers of the past. Moreover, it was assumed that these records faithfully preserved for all time an account of the true moral life for individuals and for society. Confucius had taught that it was essential to steep oneself in classical learning in order to understand the intent of the mandate of heaven.

Third, though Confucians would not put it this way, the commentary became the standard genre for explaining new ideas in the tradition. Although some of the early thinkers, especially Confucius, Mencius, and Xunzi, wrote essays without having written long commentaries, the later Confucians adopted the commentary as their standard form of exposition. They claimed Confucius as the editor of the classics rather than Confucius as the teacher in the *Analects* as their model. In fact, later Confucians would write extended commentaries on Confucius, Mencius, and Xunzi. Of course, Confucians wrote other kinds of works as well. They wrote history and poetry to go along with their commentaries on the classics. We also have wonderful collections of their correspondence with their colleagues and students, providing a rich mine of information about their ideas and lives.

The use of the commentary model has led to the stereotype of the Confucian intellectual world as one frozen forever in a reiteration of the glories of the past to the detriment of the realities of the present. Such a picture misses the point of what actually went into many of the erudite commentaries. Let us focus, as Dr. Li does so often, on the works of Zhu Xi (1130–1200), the greatest of the Southern Song Confucian philosophers.

In fact, an examination of Zhu Xi's educational program is a perfect entry into the whole question of a literati Confucian education. Now it should not surprise us that Zhu's most influential works were his famous commentaries on what he called the *Four Books*. The very category of the *Four Books* was created by Zhu Xi as part of his educational reform in the twelfth century. Zhu was concerned, as were all Confucian educators, about finding the best way to introduce students to the study of the Confucian tradition.

If the Han scholars had needed to write commentaries about the classics, then someone like Zhu living in the twelfth century believed it was even more important to provide good commentaries to students seeking the Way. Zhu, however, had a particular vision of what a good commentary should be. Of course, a responsible commentary would explain difficult grammatical issues and identify archaic terms, but, according to Zhu, this was just the preliminary task of the scholar. Along with understanding the basic grammar and sense of the text, Zhu was convinced that there was also a deeper meaning in the Confucian classics. This deeper meaning was the true intellectual and moral intent of the sages and worthies. The ancient sages and worthies did not write just to inform us about the dry facts of history, they wrote about history in order to illustrate the goals and aims of a truly moral life. In short, a good commentary should help the student to discern the concrete ways of the sages for themselves.

Where did the process of education begin? Zhu recognized that the thirteen classics were a vast sea of different genres, mixing everything from history to commentary on history and even throwing in an ancient dictionary for good measure. A student could get lost and miss the forest for the trees. Zhu stoutly maintained that the "trees" were the collected records and writings of the sages while the "forest" was the ethical meaning of the sages.

In the midst of all these materials, Zhu picked out, based on the works of his favorite Northern Song philosophers, the four key texts that he believed provided a "ladder" into the study of the whole Confucian canon. Zhu was careful to point out that his choice was just an introduction. It would be useless until and unless it was used to understand the full sweep of the Confucian heritage. In order to provide his ladder, Zhu selected four philosophic writings, namely Confucius' *Analects*, the *Mencius* (the writings of the second great Zhou Confucian, Mencius), and two excerpts from a longer ritual text, the *Great Learning* and the *Doctrine of the Mean*. Zhu's order was: The *Great Learning*, the *Analects*, the *Mencius*, and finally the *Doctrine of the Mean*.

Zhu Xi had a reason for selecting these four texts. He believed that they represented the philosophic core of the Confucian Way. Zhu was greatly criticized for his choice because he pinpointed the philosophic path as the normative one for beginning a Confucian education. As we shall see, later scholars would argue that this was too abstract a place to begin. For instance, some later Confucians argued that it was better to begin with basic rituals, a more concrete expression of the genius of the Confucian Way. Philosophy, they held, was not an essential part of the first steps in a solid Confucian education.

Zhu countered such claims by his next point in selecting these works. He truly believed that there was a core set of teachings and meanings to be found in the classics. He reasoned that it was better to try to identify these core ideas and their relevance for the student than simply to hope that the student would pick them up along the way. Zhu's plan was based on his conviction that a great deal of the Han and medieval commentary tradition was layered over the meaning of the sages making it almost impossible for a student to figure out how to interpret the texts. In short, Zhu agreed with his Northern Song masters that the real meaning of the Confucian Way had been obscured or even lost amid the vast verbiage of the older Han and Tang traditions. The loss of the true meaning of the sages was one reason, Zhu believed, for the fascination of Chinese people in the medieval period with Daoism and Buddhism. Though Zhu believed that Daoism and Buddhism were wrong in their orientation to life and the world, they did provide people with a realm of meaning that made a certain amount of sense, especially when Confucians had nothing to offer in the place of Daoist and Buddhist theories.

Zhu Xi's plan was to write commentaries on the *Four Books* based on the philosophy of the Northern Song masters. It was Zhu's conviction that the Northern Song masters had been able to cut through the mistakes of the Han and medieval periods and return to the truth of the Confucian Way. Zhu honored his favorite Northern Song masters as revivers of the Way. Of course, there was a great deal of criticism of Zhu's methods. Oddly enough, most of the critique was directed towards his philosophic interpretation rather than the basic goal of his educational reform. Confucians agreed that there had to be a place to start learning about their tradition. Zhu's curriculum remained the standard from 1313 to 1905 because it achieved its purpose. Along with Zhu's other writings, it provides the access of a ladder into the history of Confucian thought and daily life.

The reasons for Zhu's success were debated endlessly after his death. But some things were clear. In the first place, whether you agreed with him or not, Zhu *did write clearly*. Such clarity of exposition mattered a great deal in a tradition that had not always made a virtue of such clarity of thought and expression. One of the great reforms that had been begun in the late Tang by Han Yu was an appeal to write less obscure prose. One of the propensities of the Han and medieval tradition that irked the late Tang and Song reformers was the overuse of highly complex forms of writing. For instance, many writers sought to demonstrate their mastery of the tradition by writing convoluted prose laced with esoteric terminology. In a language using characters for words rather than an alphabet, it was easy to find strange and ancient expressions and turns of phrases that hardly anyone would understand without an elaborate commentary.

Following Han Yu, Zhu and the other Song Confucians rebelled against the elaborate writing styles of the medieval Confucian world. In fact, modern linguists have pointed out that Zhu Xi actually went quite a long way by writing in what can only be called a vernacular style. Although his writings are still considered part of the grand tradition of the literary language, he tried to make this language as user-friendly as possible. Rather than mystifying an idea or interpretation of the classics as a pose for learning, Zhu believed that a good teacher should explain as clearly as possible what was going on in the text. Of course, Zhu could be as complicated as any great philosopher, but his desire was to communicate with his students. To this end, Master Zhu commented on the various basic textbooks for children such as the *Elementary Learning* and the *Three Character Classic*.

Along with his commentaries, Zhu and a good friend Lü Zuqian, also wrote another text called *Reflections on Things at Hand* to serve as a step stool to the ladder of the Four Books. The *Reflections* was a masterful anthology of the writings of the four Northern Song philosophers mixed with Zhu's own commentary on the selections. Over the centuries this book became the source of philosophic inspiration for generations of Chinese, Korean, and Japanese students. The whole purpose of the anthology was to explain the true meaning of the teachings of the sages from philosophic speculation to the conduct of daily life and family ritual. As we shall see in later chapters, Zhu was also the author of a highly respected collection of rituals for daily life. This ritual text was also a guidebook for the Li family. In short, Master Zhu had attempted to provide materials for the education of Confucian scholars.

Actually, as we shall see later in this chapter, Zhu's commentaries and philosophic writings were not precisely where the children began their education. There was the need to master a great deal of the Chinese written language and the history of Chinese culture before even the most precocious youth could tackle Zhu's writings. There were a number of favorite texts used by teachers over the centuries to introduce the richness of the classical heritage to children.

The Chinese language has an unbroken history going back to the dynasties before the Zhou. However, from the very beginning the written form appears to have diverged from the spoken language. As time went on, there developed a standard literary language and various spoken forms. All are called Chinese, but in the case of the spoken language, it developed many different dialects. Although many of these dialects were mutually unintelligible, because of the use of the ubiquitous Chinese characters, anyone who learned the written language could communicate with anyone else throughout the empire. Countless generations of Chinese children learned their literary Chinese from studying the Confucian classics. Authors such as Mencius were held up as paragons not only of philosophy but also of prose style.

Along with learning literary Chinese, youths were also introduced to the glories of Chinese poetry. One of the basic Confucian classics was the *Book of Poetry*, a collection of poems that was already old by the time of Confucius. This anthology of early Chinese poetry contained some of the most ancient writings preserved anywhere in the world. An educated person was expected to be able to write poetry. Of course, not everyone was good at it, but it was an art that the Confucians took seriously. By the later dynasties such as the Ming and Qing, women contributed brilliant efforts to the Chinese poetic tradition. Mrs. Li was an accomplished poet and a member of an exclusive club of educated women dedicated to writing, reading, and commenting on poetry.

EDUCATION AS CULTIVATION

Confucian culture was held together by a commitment to the mastery of a defined classical canon. In fact, one of the ways to figure out a person's intellectual affiliation in imperial China was to discover what canonical tradition he or she was committed to as a means of education and cultivation. Of course, as we have seen and will see, anyone who aspired to literati status had to have had a Confucian education. Many Buddhist monks and Daoist priests were as proud of their Confucian learning as any high government official. Confucian learning was the common coin of the realm.

The Confucian fixation with the texts of the tradition served to define who was and was not a Confucian. Anybody was part of the Confucian tradition who took the canon as the guide for life. You could be a mystic, a great philosopher, a drunken and brilliant poet, a refined lady, a humble village teacher, a great civil engineer – what bound all these people together were the multiple threads of the canonical tradition. Sometimes people wonder how everyone fitted under the Confucian tent. The answer is that they became Confucians by education and commitment. Education was the entrance requirement for anyone who wished to be considered part of the Confucian family.

Some Confucians were nervous about this reliance on texts. The great Ming dynasty critic of Zhu Xi, Wang Yangming, believed that people could get lost in the texts. Moreover, just reading and memorizing the Confucian classics did not mean understanding them, much less that the precepts would become a model for living. For Wang the real test of being an authentic Confucian was to fuse knowledge and action into a moral life. Master Zhu would have agreed completely about the need to make the texts one's own.

While mastery of the texts was a necessary feature of Confucian identity, it was not a sufficient definition by itself. The Song, Ming, and Qing scholars all stressed the need for a level of commitment to the Confucian way of life that went far beyond the mere ability to read the texts. This was just the first step in the education of a Confucian. The second step was to learn how to make use of the texts. Master Zhu used all kinds of methods to encourage this deep appreciation of the canon. He developed a whole art of reading, reflecting, and meditating that was aimed at just such a rich discernment of the Confucian Way. For instance, he talked about reading the texts as literally eating them. You had to ingest their meaning via your reading for them to become living texts and not just inanimate words.

The great Confucians stressed the role of sincere effort and self-cultivation as the second step of education. They were aware that not all brilliant minds could make this step from mere scholarship to a commitment of the mind-heart to action modeled on the sages and worthies. They were also aware that sometimes simple and less educated people, moved by the moral message of the Confucian Way would actually embody the living ethical virtues better than a scholar who was merely interested in fame and fortune. Confucius himself had taught that among the people in a village he could find teachers.

Because the road to wealth and fame did lie in later imperial China along the path of Confucian education, the possibilities for spiritual and moral fakery were endless. Generations of Chinese novelists wrote with blinding clarity about the foibles of the Confucian world. The image of the Confucian as a bumbling fool or a corrupt official without one ounce of virtue is not merely a picture of the Confucian past. Generations of sincere Confucians were aware of the multiple levels of hypocrisy embedded in the search for wealth and power. According to the true scholars of the tradition, nothing in it was worthwhile if it did not induce a reformation of the human character. The ultimate aim of Confucian education was not merely erudition, though Chinese scholars did admire erudition and genius as things of worth; it was the morality and personal integrity that flowed from the real study of the Confucian canon.

A perfect example of the preliminary fusion of language learning and Confucian ethical education was happening with the two oldest children of the Lis. They were in the midst of studying and memorizing the *Classic of Filial Piety*. This was a very short text with only eighteen chapters, and each chapter was no longer than an extended paragraph. However, the *Classic of Filial Piety* was a text that children had memorized and reflected on for hundreds of years. It taught, via exposition of principles and examples, about one of the central Confucian virtues, filial piety.

Along with the five classic virtues of humaneness, righteousness, civility (ritual propriety), wisdom, and faithfulness, filial piety or *hsiao* was an essential Confucian virtue. The philosophical and sociological reasons were clear to anyone who thought about Confucianism in particular and Chinese culture in general. It has been a common observation that all Chinese culture revolves around the family. A person is only a person within the family. Moreover, the metaphor of the family is then extended to the larger social world. For instance, from the very beginning of Chinese civilization the rulers were likened to the fathers and mothers of the country. The family was the matrix of culture and the apex of family virtues was filial piety.

It was important to remember that filial piety is a complex virtue. All too often people believed that it meant blind obedience first to one's family elders and then to anyone else in authority. But this was to misunderstand the reciprocal nature of filial piety. Although deference and respect were at the heart of filial piety, these were virtues that were built on a social foundation of reciprocal relationships of affection and love. For instance, the Confucians argued that, in an ideal sense, we love and revere our parents because they first loved us, as did their parents, and so forth. One of the things that a truly filial child owes his or her parents is honesty, without which no social or family relationship can grow.

In fact, the fifth of the cardinal virtues was faithfulness or *xin*. The linked social relationship was friendship. Faithfulness meant that people should stand by their words and deeds. They should be stalwart supporters of friends and family. Of course, such faithfulness had to be directed by a sense of humanity and righteousness and needed to be wisely carried out in a ritually satisfactory manner. Especially within the family ritual was important to help people deal with each other in a humane way. But when righteousness was violated, then it was the responsibility of a filial child or a spouse to remonstrate with the friend, spouse, or kin. It was a case, using a metaphor drawn from the Christian tradition, of hating the sin but still loving the sinner. Because remonstration within the family was so potentially disruptive of the family and social order, Confucians counseled that it should only be used as a last resort. Nonetheless, it was a resort that was owed even to a mother or to a father in love and concern for their ultimate well-being.

Mrs. Li, as would have generations of educated Confucian mothers, had instructed all of her children in the spirit of filial piety by introducing them to the eighteen sections of the *Classic of Filial Piety*. The classic began with a picture of Confucius speaking at leisure to one of his famous disciples, Tseng Tzu. Confucius began with the comment that the early sage kings were rulers of the world because they had the most perfected virtue or power, the famous notion of *de*, and the most refined *Dao* or correct Way. The reason that we can tell they had both virtue and the Way was that society was so well ordered and harmonious. Confucius wrote that "Filiality is the foundation of virtue and the root of civilization" (Makra 1961, p.3). Confucius then provided some examples of how we must act with filiality in order to accord with the Way. The teaching continues with the important admonition: "Thus, begun in the service of our parents, continued in service to the prince, filiality is completed in the building up of our character" (1961, p.3). Confucius ended the first section on filial piety by quoting the *Book of Poetry* that "Ever think of your ancestors/ Cultivating their virtue" (1961, p.3).

The linkage is highlighted between the family, the social order, and our personal self-cultivation. Although filial piety is the most familial of the major Confucian virtues, the *Classic of Filial Piety*'s second section immediately discusses the role of the ruler's commitment to filial piety. The text plays upon one common name for paramount Chinese rulers, namely the "son of heaven." In this fashion the link between persons within a family setting is continued for the emperor because he too is linked to heaven as a son to a father. As the text says, "He who loves his parents does not dare to hate others. He who reverences his parents does not dare to act contemptuously toward others" (1961, p.5).

Confucian students will immediately recognize this teaching as a rephrasing of the Confucian version of the golden rule. What is distinctive about the Confucian version is that it is often done in the negative rather than the positive mode. Some Confucian scholars have suggested that by phrasing the golden rule in this fashion Confucius was being cautious in giving too much moral advice. Rather than listing all kinds of positive injunction that could be mistakenly applied to other people, Confucius suggested a simpler way to check on our moral actions. We need to ask, would we like other people to treat us like this? How would we like to be treated? The positive teaching embedded here is that we should not dare to hate other people. In terms of the ruler, Confucius states that "By love and reverence being perfectly fulfilled in the service to his parents, his moral influence is shed upon the people and he becomes a pattern for all the border nations" (1961, p.5).

The structure of filial piety is resolutely social in nature. In order to be filial we must ask about the feelings not only of ourselves but also for others. There is a predilection for empathy for others built into the whole edifice of filiality. Such a regimen of moral cultivation does not encourage solitary meditation on perfection that cannot be shared with other people. Moreover, the true ruler is governed by love and reverence for parents and the common people. Even the most powerful person in the empire is subject to moral constraints. In fact, Confucians did argue that the emperor perhaps had an even greater need of moral cultivation because he was to be a pattern for all the nations. In the Song dynasty the emperors were reported to have tried to avoid their Confucian tutors because they were tired of being endlessly reminded of the need for the cultivation of their virtues. Power, social relations, and virtue were connected by filiality in the most primordial and intimate terms.

After the second section on the son of heaven, the *Classic of Filial Piety* spells out the duties of princes, high officers, scholars, and the common people. If the highest ruler is the son of heaven, the text teaches that the common people have an obligation to follow the way of heaven. Heaven or *tian* is described, within a few short paragraphs, both in terms of an order of the world and as a filial relationship of a father and a son. Although the common people are not directly related to heaven, for that is the prerogative of the son of heaven, they are still linked to the cosmos by the way of heaven. In the classical Chinese state cult, it was only the emperor who could sacrifice upon the altar of heaven to heaven itself. He did so as the son of heaven just as other sons reverenced and loved their own fathers. The emperor was the chief priest of the empire; he also had the obligation to live within the way of heaven just as all other people were so obligated. "So it is that, from the Son of Heaven to the commoners, if filial piety is not pursued from beginning to end, disasters are sure to follow" (1961, p.13).

The whole doctrine of filial piety is a wonderful example of what scholars call the correlative nature of the Confucian worldview. Everything is linked to everything else, though some things are more important and more influential than others. Mrs. Li would make this point by telling her children about the Confucian quarrel with another early Chinese philosopher, Mozi. Mozi might well have started out as a Confucian, but very soon he turned on the Confucians of his day and developed his own philosophy.

Two things about Mo Tzu bothered the Confucians mightily. The first was Mozi's argument that the only way we can judge any virtue or action is by the pragmatic principle of the highest good. Furthermore, Mozi claimed that only useful things are truly good things. The Confucians disagreed. Some things might not be economically useful in a purely utilitarian sense, but were good nonetheless. Poetry and loving rituals were the kinds of things that the Confucians defended against the powerful logic of Mozi's utilitarian appeal.

The second thing that outraged Confucians was Mozi's idea that we should love each and every person equally. This was his famous doctrine of universal love. Now, Confucians were not uninterested in love, but they believed that it was unrealistic to demand that we love everyone equally. This went against the notion of filial piety as derived from the family; moreover, such lack of discernment of social location meant that we were liable to forget the levels of obligations we owed to different people. Of course, the Confucians balanced their sense of filial piety as a familial virtue with a strong commitment to social justice founded on the virtue of righteousness, but they never wavered from their conviction that we begin and are grounded in our families. We simply will never learn to love everyone the same. This would be a waste of time and would deflect our energies away from the more useful cultivation of filial piety based on humaneness. Mrs. Li would reinforce the teaching of Confucian reciprocal affection by reminding her children that they had obligations to those outside the family, indeed to the most distant nations, based on the firm foundation of the filial piety that they learned within their own family.

In the ninth section of the classic, the connection between the life of the family and the governance of the empire is made explicit. "The sage, because of his example of reverence for his parents, taught love. The teaching of the sage, even though not severe, was efficacious. His rule, without being strict, was effective" (1961, p.19). Just slightly later the classic taught that "The relation between father and son is rooted in nature and develops into the proper relation between prince and minister" (1961, p.21). As Mrs. Li explained to her children, the family and the empire were linked together through the virtue of filial piety.

She went on to give a different example of the reach of filial piety. One of the most common elements of Chinese cosmology was embedded in the theory of the five phases. The foundation of all things was their allotment of qi or vital force, and vital force itself was always rhythmic in nature. The vital force oscillated between yin and yang, the strong and the weak, the light and the dark, the young and the old, the male and the female. Yet yin and yang could never be separated for a moment. They were always part of each other. When yang reached its outer limit of maturation, then yin was sure to set in. When yin became dominant, then yang would arise again.

Another way to see the rhythm of yin and yang within the vital force that was allotted to each thing or person was to understand its balance of the five phases. These were the phases of wood, fire, earth, metal, and water. They could be mixed in a myriad of combinations and metaphorically represented everything from tastes to moral virtues. What was important to remember was that they were not to be thought of as substances in their own right but rather as actions, processes, or phases of the vital force.

The question of the five phases had first come up when one of Mrs. Li's daughters asked about why different dynasties used different colors to symbolize their rule and how these colors were chosen. It was a perfect question to explain the five phases. In fact, there had been major debates about the question of color in the founding of some dynasties. The theory was this. Just as with people, dynasties move in a life cycle from youth to old age. While there is nothing deterministic about how long a dynasty will endure, it is the case that at some time the dynasty will grow old. This is sad, but it is a fact of nature.

Each dynasty had a favorite color that expresses its virtue in regard to the previous dynasty. Moreover, the phases themselves moved in a certain pattern relative to each other. For instance, fire could melt metal, and metal could cut wood. Therefore, if a "metal" dynasty was to replace a "wood" dynasty, then its characteristic colors should be changed as well in terms of its ritual vestments and so forth. The color of metal was white and the color of wood was green. It was sometimes a complicated pattern, yet a pattern nonetheless. It was for this reason that the first emperor Qin chose black as the color of water to distinguish his empire from the red color of the Zhou dynasty.

The number of five was repeated over and over again in classifying the patterns of Confucian life. Mrs. Li pointed out that there were, of course, five cardinal virtues, namely humaneness, righteousness, civility, wisdom, and faithfulness. Each of these in turn was correlated to a specific emotional state such as fire being related to the feeling of joy. Filial piety was the kind of virtue that had to embody all of the five virtues perfectly in order to be a true virtue. Mrs. Li wanted to make sure that the children understood the correlated nature of the world and the virtues.

The question first arose through the study of the fourteenth section of the classic. Confucius taught that "The gentleman's service to his parents is filial; his fidelity can be transferred to his prince" (1961, p.31). The key to understanding how to be filial revolved around the proper understanding of fidelity. The term could also be understood as constant, loyal, honest, or sincere. Confucius had also taught that this was one of the two threads that held his whole teaching together. It was the sense of faithfulness to another based on reciprocal empathy. It could also be said to symbolize the inner and outer, the yin and yang dimensions of human conduct. A person needed to be faithful to both the family and the larger world. In fact, such a reciprocal faithfulness was part of what Confucius taught about the reality of ultimate humaneness as the basis of the Confucian moral order.

The fifteenth section of the classic was a very important and difficult one to understand within the parameters of a Confucian family. It was the duty of correction that a son owed his father. The dialogue between Zengzi and Confucius began by Zengzi asking the following question, "Dare I ask if a son, by obeying all of his father's commands, can be called filial?"(1961, p.33). Of course, there is a great deal of logic and Chinese family behavior behind this question. On the whole, it was considered moral for a son to obey his father in all things, and for a daughter to listen carefully to what her mother taught.

Confucius, however, answered, "What kind of talk is this?" (ibid.). The Master immediately analogized his answer to the role of the Son of Heaven, the emperor, with his ministers. If the emperor had seven true ministers, Confucius argued, then the ruler could never lose the empire. Why? Because one of the roles of the good minister was to advise the emperor about his conduct and policy. And such advice could not be limited to merely telling the emperor everything he wanted to hear. Even if the emperor were imperfect, he could be a highly successful ruler if he would listen to his ministers' advice about the imperfections.

Confucius went on to teach that, "If an officer has one friend to correct him, he would not lose his good name. If a father had one son to reason with him, he would not be engulfed in a moral wrong"(ibid.). Confucius concluded with this comment, "In short, when there is a question of moral wrong, there should be correction. How can you say that filiality consists in simply obeying a father?"(ibid.). Of course, there were hedges around arguing too much with one's father and mother. What is being talked about is real moral evil. This places a great burden on the son or daughter.

In order to be a filial son or daughter, the person, under the obligation of correcting the parent, must first know the difference between right and wrong, and between civility and impropriety. Just arguing with one's parents because one does not feel that they are right, or because they are giving a distasteful order, is not enough. One must have cultivated one's own character to the point of certainty about the moral principles involved. Furthermore, one must then "reason" with the parent. There is a demand for civility even when remonstrating with parents or social superiors.

There was a summary of the five virtues called the three bonds. These were the relationship of the ruler and minister, father and son, husband and wife. It was argued that the three bonds were nothing but fetters for the minister, son, and wife. The only proper action for the minister, the son, and the wife was complete obedience to the ruler, father, and husband. However, Mrs. Li noted that in the earliest formulation of the famous theory of the three bonds, as in the *Classic of Filial Piety*, there was a clear teaching of the necessity of remonstration and correction. When a ruler, a father, and a husband acted incorrectly and this imperfection touched on a real moral failure or oversight, then true morality demanded that the minister, the son, or the wife remonstrate with the ruler, father, or husband.

But what if the superior does not heed the advice given in affection and moral concern? What is the minister, the son, or the wife to do? This is a very difficult question. For the minister the ultimate choice would be to withdraw from government service. However, this was possibly a dangerous act because a resignation and withdrawal from office would certainly be interpreted as a moral censure of the ruler. And rulers did not like to be censured by their ministers. Mrs. Li, with some humor, pointed out that when an official resigned, the most common excuse was illness. This was a much safer way to withdraw than to confront the ruler with his moral or intellectual failings.

PREPARING FOR THE EXAMINATIONS

Dr. Li was also concerned about the preparation of his sons for the three levels of the examination system. They had been tutored at home by Mrs. Li and a fine local school teacher, but it was now time to find a private tutor to continue their education. The selection of a tutor was an important task for Dr. Li. It was doubly important because the Li's took their Confucianism seriously. It was not merely a matter of preparing for the examinations. There were special schools and publications that were geared to teaching the technical skills necessary to pass the examinations.

The Li's were of the opinion that merely viewing the examinations as a technical, pragmatic exercise was a mistake. While it was true that there was no way to make the educational process easy or even particularly enjoyable, it was crucial to remember that the aim of education was the cultivation of the self. If the moral purpose of the examinations was lost, the Confucian way itself was lost. There had to be a balance between studying for the examinations themselves and learning about the Confucian way.

The fundamental body of material that had to be mastered was the Confucian canon itself. By the Song dynasty this had grown to thirteen in number. Any candidate had to have a working familiarity with the whole canon. In many cases, this meant that the student had to memorize huge sections of the classics. The reason for this was twofold. In the examinations a student would often be given a short phrase from one of the classics. Before commenting on the meaning of the phrase, the student was expected to write out the longer passage around the short phrase. It was a given that the student knew the text and could reproduce it without error. Only after the student's memory was tested was the student allowed to give the answer to the question itself. The questions could be over a host of issues including philology, philosophy, poetic theory, history, and governmental policy.

The great Zhu Xi passed the imperial examinations when he was eighteen. The average age of his class was thirty-five. This showed what a genius Zhu Xi was and just how difficult it was to pass all the examinations. Years of careful study and preparation were necessary for success. Although Confucius had not been thinking about the examinations when he invented the role of a Confucian teacher, it was crucial that people had a realistic chance of passing the examinations.

After the crucial stage of memorization, there was the stage of interpretation. There was no way to make the memorization easy or pleasant. Many people did not have the endurance or talent to memorize. But generations of Chinese teachers, often through the endless task of repetitions and practice, had been able to fill the minds of their young and not so young charges with the requisite body of memorized texts. Then the second stage began.

Generally Confucian educators suggested a three-stage approach to teaching. The first was the work that needed to be done at home before a child started formal education at around eight years of age. At this age boys and girls would be schooled together in the various recognized elementary texts such as the *Three Thousand Character Classic*. The second stage was from eight to fifteen years of age. Boys and girls would be separated and the sons would be taught at a school or by a private tutor. It was at this age that the student would be introduced to the core of the Confucian classics. It was a crucial time to memorize and begin to understand the broad range of Confucian learning. The third stage would begin when the boy was fifteen and would extend, ideally, to the age of around twenty-two. It was at this stage that the young man would be introduced to the commentaries of Zhu Xi. It was also at this stage that a student would begin a more rigorous study of Chinese history as understood by Confucian teachers.

It was at the second stage of learning, what the Confucians called the learning of the adult, that a good teacher was essential. The teacher needed to be firm yet humane. There was no way to make the examination-based curriculum a real joy. However, a good teacher could make it something less than a pedagogical disaster. This meant that the tutor had to have some kind of vision of the Confucian Way beyond iron discipline and punishment, although those twin rods were necessary from time to time even with the brightest and best student.

Many tutors at the more advanced level were men who had passed the lower levels of the examination system. In the present case, the tutor candidate, after passing the local and provincial examinations, had failed at the national level three times. There was no disgrace in such a failure; though the toll it took on the mind-heart of the candidate was hard to measure. It turned many men into embittered people. This was one reason that Dr. Li wanted to get to know the candidate. Such bitterness was not something that needed to be passed along to his children. Moreover, giving in to bitterness showed a lack of proper Confucian self-cultivation.

One of the most important things to be drawn from the life of Confucius was the teaching that worldly success was not the ultimate measure of human life. Confucius believed that he had failed in renewing his society, yet he was counted one of the foremost sages. Faithfulness to the task and a balanced personality were the aim of education for the person. The role of a teacher was a worthy one and this candidate had all of these qualities. The prospective teacher of Dr. Li's children was well regarded as a local scholar and was considered a fine calligrapher and poet. These were two arts that also needed to be taught well. A student was expected to understand how to write poetry and to do so in a decent hand.

Along with prodigious feats of memory, the student was expected to understand the texts. This understanding was historical, procedural, and philosophical. Besides the history of China, the student was also expected to know a great deal about the form of government and how it worked. This was important because one of the prime features of the examination system was the recruitment for the imperial civil service. But before the student was asked to give policy advice, he was expected to show that he was philosophically literate.

In 1313 the interpretations of Master Zhu had been made the standard for the examinations. The student needed to be conversant with the canon as interpreted and expounded by Zhu Xi in his numerous commentaries. But as with so many literate traditions, there developed a canon within a canon. Theoretically, all the classics were important, however, some classics were used, in Zhu's metaphor, as ladders to the other classics. From Zhu's day on this meant the famous *Four Books* (the *Great Learning*, the *Analects*, the *Mencius*, and the *Doctrine of the*

Mean). In some ways this was a blessing for the student. It gave them a secure place to start. They did not have to learn the whole history of Chinese thought in the same way that they had mastered the canon itself. They were given a focus through the lens of Master Zhu's commentaries on the *Four Books*.

The candidate tutor also suggested that he would make use of an extended commentary on the *Four Books* that added more of Master Zhu's comments on the basic texts. This extended commentary, also from the Song period, reproduced Zhu's commentaries and then added additional commentary on each passage drawn from Zhu's other works that were germane to the commentary on the *Four Books*. If this sounds complicated, it makes more sense when you look at the written page. The text of the classic is printed in larger print, followed by the main commentaries of Master Zhu. Then the editor added smaller and smaller print for at least two more levels of commentary. In all there were three levels of printing. The smallest characters were quoted from Master Zhu's correspondence with friends, other commentaries, and from his collected dialogues with his students. The tutor believed that this would help Dr. Li's sons master different commentaries while learning more about Master Zhu's own interpretations.

Learning to read commentaries was a crucial part of a Confucian education in the late imperial period. In fact, it could be argued that the examinations themselves were a huge test in writing commentaries on the examinations themselves. Candidates had to be able to follow perfectly the set format for the questions and how they were to be answered. Although individual creativity was acceptable, it could only be added on top of the basic information about the texts. The examiners were more interested in education than individual genius. The best way to show one's skill was to build on the works of the accepted scholarly authorities.

There were even more basic ways to begin this part of the preparations. The tutor candidate suggested that it would also be wise to introduce the great *Reflections on Things at Hand* at this stage of the education. Along with the six hundred and twenty-two selections, Master Zhu also added his own comments about how to interpret the Northern Song masters. The anthology was organized into fourteen chapters, each of which introduced an important topic for Confucian learning. These ranged from discussions of the substance of the Way to the dispositions of the sages and worthies. It also included practical advice about when to serve or not to serve, and when to advance or withdraw from public service. It also touched on educational theory, preserving one's nature, correcting mistakes and improving oneself, and regulating the family. In short, it was a textbook for Master Zhu's vision of Confucian self-cultivation, education, family life, social service, history, and an analysis of false doctrine.

TEACHERS OF THE INNER QUARTERS

Education had always been essential to the lives of young Confucian men. From the beginning it made them members of the historical lineage that stretched from the early sages to Confucius and the other Zhou masters, to the Han scholastics, and the revivers of the Tang, Song, and Ming dynasties. However, as the centuries rolled on, education became more and more important for women as well. While Dr. Li was interviewing potential male tutors, Mrs. Li was doing the same thing for her daughters. She was searching, as would have been said at the time, for a teacher of the "inner quarters." The inner quarters referred to the part of the house that was reserved solely for women to use. Because of this social custom, only women could serve as teachers for other women.

By the Ming dynasty it had become common for women to receive more than a smattering of a Confucian education. Though not nearly as long as those of their brothers, many young Confucian women became passably proficient in some of the Confucian arts. There was actually a long tradition about the role of the educated woman in Confucian lore. The mothers of Confucius and Mencius were revered as the first teachers of the greatest of Chinese teachers. In both cases these young widows took an active role in the education of their sons. They taught their sons and were models of Confucian deportment and virtues that were remembered by generations of Confucians. In the Han dynasty there was the example of Ban Zhao (45–115 C.E.), a great historian who first assisted her brother (Ban Gu) with the writing of *Han shu* (History of the Han) and later completed it when her brother died. She was venerated as one of the greatest of Chinese historians. As we shall see, Ban Zhao also wrote works specifically about the education of women. In the early medieval period we learn of many educated Confucian women who urged their sons, husbands, and fathers on to better lives.

In the medieval period, though a good Confucian like Mrs. Li would not give it too much thought, many Daoist texts were revealed not to men but to aristocratic women, and in excellent classical Chinese at that. In fact, the Daoist tradition, both in its great early philosophic texts and in its later religious revelations, always remembered the role of the feminine in the cultivation of the self. When great famines swept through the country and people were prone to sell or even kill their daughters out of desperation to save the rest of the family, the Daoist reminded people that without women the world would become unbalanced. There was also a tradition of learning for Buddhist nuns, who often became the friends of married women and took part in the educated life of women in imperial China.

In the Northern Song, two of the most famous Neo-Confucian philosophers were part of the chain of Confucians educated by their mothers from an early age. Cheng Hao (1032–85) and Cheng Yi (1033–1107) were the most famous pair of philosopher-brothers in the history of Chinese thought, and they too were first educated by a young widowed mother who was devoted to their education. Other less famous scholars over the centuries also told stories about how they had learned their first texts and Confucian precepts from their mothers.

In short, there was no lack of examples of educated women in the history of Confucian China. In fact, educated women could point out that in the Confucian classics there were many examples of women who used their wits to assist their families. Women often saved their brothers, fathers, and sons from disasters through the skilled use of reason and historical analogy.

However, it was also obvious that the role of women had declined from the early days into the Song, Ming, and Qing times. There are many reasons for this, and some of the blame must be placed on the shoulders of the Neo-Confucians themselves. Other blame can be shared more generously through the historic transformations of Chinese culture from the Zhou, Han and Tang periods (c. 550 B.C.E. to 906 C.E.) to the Song, Yuan, Ming, and Qing dynasties (960–1911). One of the reasons for the decline, and this was not unique to China during this period, was the transformation of Chinese society from an aristocratic world to the world of literati Confucian bureaucrats recruited via the civil service examinations.

Without putting too fine a point on it, aristocratic Chinese women appeared to have had more freedom than the later women of the literati classes. Although it is usually false to use European class labels to describe Chinese society, it is true that early and medieval China was dominated by a landed aristocracy. At the top the emperor ruled and reigned with the aid of his clan. There was also a large collection of powerful families who owned great estates and even controlled small armies. In time of trouble, just like in Europe, these noble families dominated Chinese life in the countryside as well as at court. As the court became less and less powerful, the great landed families of the North China plain grew in strength.

Although during the Han the institution of examinations as a method to select officials had been put into effect, the examinations were only one way to office. The more common way was by recommendation based on family connections. The great landed families dominated the government as they did all aspects of Chinese society. However, a subtle shift began with the fall of the Han dynasty. The unifications of the Qin and Han period permanently transformed China. For instance, the empire of Han provided an unforgettable model of what China ought to be. The model was one of unity. Only a unified country was a proper country.

Because of the model of unification, all the various periods of disunity that followed from the fall of the Han empire in the third century were viewed as aberrations. The dream was of a single country. What was truly amazing was the fact that the dream was often the reality. China was able to remain a unified country for much longer than any other nation or group of nations in the world. There have been larger empires than China, but there has never been such a large country that has been able to maintain unity over such a long period of time and over such a great expanse of territory.

What allowed the Chinese empire to flourish while the Romans, who ruled a similar sized empire at the other end of Eurasia, became a mere classical dream for the European world? No one can give a coherent answer to this question. However, there are a number of points that can be adduced for extended success of the Chinese experiment. The first has to do with the homogeneity of Chinese culture. The Confucians called their cultural heritage "this culture of ours." It was the obligation of a Confucian to revere and pass this culture on. The Confucians had a filial responsibility not only to their kin but to the culture that nurtured them. Confucian scholars would lovingly preserve their culture and, as was the case with the great Song revival and with the Evidential Research School of the Qing, even add to the patrimony in creative ways.

So one reason for the longevity of the Chinese state was Confucian cultural bonds. This had become orthodoxy in the Han empire when Emperor Wu declared Confucianism the basis for government. One reason for the choice of Confucianism – especially from the Confucian perspective – was that it trod a middle path between the other ideological possibilities of the time. On the one hand there was the great Legalist school that had helped the Qin first unify all under heaven. However, the Legalists were forever frowned upon because their policies were too authoritarian and constrictive. The Legalists helped to conquer an empire but they proved unable to rule it for long. At the other end of the spectrum was the revived philosophic Daoism known as the teaching of Huang-Lao after the culture heroes of the Yellow Emperor and Lao Zi, the author of the *Dao de jing*. The Huang-Lao school argued for a more spontaneous and relaxed form of government based on the Daoist principles of uncontrived action and even no action at all.

The Confucians offered a road between the extremes of the Legalists and Daoists. The great Han thinkers were also clever enough, though they would never have admitted it, to borrow the best points that the Legalists and Huang-Lao traditions had to offer. For instance, the Han Confucians were more than willing to make use of the imperial form of government allowing the new Han state to retain the essential structure of the unified Qin legal system, while tempering its rigidities by arguing that wise ministers ought to be able to interpret the law in terms of Confucian moral principles. This advice made great sense to the Han emperors. It facilitated the creation of a huge empire that was governed without recourse to the re-feudalization of China. Good ministers were less likely to revolt against their Confucian emperors than those powerful princes and dukes.

From the schools such as the Huang-Lao the Confucians fused their storied reverence for social morality and ritual with a comprehensive cosmological system. In short, the Han Confucians added a great deal of Daoist philosophy to their staple of Confucian ethics. Important theories such as the processes of the yin and yang forces and the five phases became part of the Han Confucian synthesis. For the first time Confucians could compete with any other philosophic school at any level. Moreover, the Confucians promised to provide an educated and loyal core of civil servants. When appointing a Confucian minister, the ruler was (fairly) certain about what he was supporting.

Added to the Confucian appropriation of Legalist and Huang-Lao elements, the Han Confucians also approved of the Qin's urge towards standardization, the second reason for China's unity. The Qin and Han empires strove to bring unity to the realm by procedures as diverse as stipulating the length of cart axles. This was as important in its own way as the fixing of the gauge of railroad tracks. The reason for this was that if you had the same length axles then the paths cut across the country-side would be easy for any cart to follow. This was especially important in North China because of the composition of the famous yellow earth, which rutted easily in the rain and then dried out into deep tracks. The Han also used the standardized Qin version of Chinese writing. The very nature of Chinese writing, the use of what are called characters, made communication via literature possible across and among different dialect groups. Unlike Europe with its many languages, China had one written language. There was even a common language called Mandarin based on the dialect of the region around Beijing. Officials needed to speak this lingua franca when they joined the civil service. Although it had not been invented to do so, the visual uniformity of Chinese characters helped to bind the culture together.

Added to all of this was the fundamental Confucian inclination towards unity. This was expressed in the hope for a just and harmonious family, society, state, and world. Confucians could be accused of prizing harmony even above consideration of justice or anything else. This notion of harmony stretched the limits of empire. The ideal state was one at peace and unified under one dynasty.

There were some breaks in this ideal picture, the longest being the gap between the end of the Han dynasty in the third century and the con-solidation of the Tang dynasty in the seventh. This long period of dis-unity was disturbing to the Confucian historians. It also marked another important transition. North China was dominated for these centuries by a series of dynasties with non-Chinese ruling houses. The perennial Chinese fear that if the empire were not strong then the northern, eastern, and western barbarians would seize regions of China was proved by the Han-Tang interregnum. Nonetheless, south China, that is to say the region around the great Yangtze, was controlled even in the period of turmoil by a succession of Chinese states. Many important northern families fled the constant warfare and barbarian rule to live in the south. At this period, the middle part of China became firmly Chinese, as the ethnic Chinese immigrants pushed the tribal peoples further and further out of the productive lands into the mountains and forests of the south.

Yet the southern Chinese maintained the dream of unity. And as the northern dynasties were slowly assimilated into the Chinese world through long rule and intermarriage, they too plotted for conquest of all of China. When this finally happened with the founding of the Tang dynasty in 618, China was reunited into an even larger empire. Most Chinese historians grade the Tang as the greatest of Chinese dynasties in terms of its cultural and military success.

A far-reaching cultural transformation accompanied the transfer of the center of economic gravity from the north to the south. By the Northern Song the change was complete. We find Northern Song writings recording debates between the older northern members of the great families and the newly recruited southerners. The southern men came from new families in the sense that many of them became government officials because of the examinations. Many southern officials were the first members of their families to play a role on the national stage. They owed their success to the patronage of the emperor and not the extended power of their ancient families. This was a dramatic shift in power in the capital that did not go unnoticed by the older northerners.

This shift of power in the Northern Song was completed with the conquest of half of China by the barbarian Jin dynasty. The Song had allied themselves with the Jin against the other northern barbarian dynasty, and while the Jin were completely successful in their campaign, the Song military adventure was a failure. The Jin, therefore, saw no reason not to try to wrest all of China from the Song. The Jin almost succeeded and all of the north China plain, the heart of classical China, was lost. The Southern Song dynasty moved its capital into the Yangtse basin and even paid tribute to its Jin neighbors. To get around the disunity of the empire, the Song adopted the pretense that this was only a temporary setback and that they would reconquer the north. The Song never did regain the north and was finally completely destroyed by the new Mongol empire.

One of the things that happened during this shift in power from the north to the south was the loss of status for women. The reasons for this are not entirely clear beyond the fact that, at least for the upper classes, aristocratic societies usually allow modicums of power to elite women. This was not the case in practice or theory for the post-Song literati world. Although the literati families were definitely an elite, they were not always great landholders. In any event, their power was given to them by their success in the examinations.

The main reason that the Neo-Confucian philosophers gave for this downgrading of the role of women was the view that women were purportedly unable to use reason as well as men. Furthermore, women were considered to be more driven by their emotions and were hence unfit to take part in life beyond their own families. This kind of thinking also had practical ramifications for women's lives. The post-Song period was also governed by the philosophic opinion that a woman should not remarry; all too many young women were relegated to widowhood at an early age because of the new theory about female virtue.

However, educated women did find outlets for their mind-hearts. Poetry was one area in which women were allowed and even encouraged to play a role. Chinese women had been poets ever since the earliest times and the women of late imperial China continued this pastime. Mrs. Li, for instance, would review the teacher's poetry as one key factor in choosing an educator for her daughters.

The educated women of the Ming and Qing period actually turned the male conceit that they were governed more by feeling than reason to philosophic advantage. The women knew that Confucians had determined that even the sage had feelings. This was a theory about human nature that separated Confucians from Buddhists and Daoists. Confucians argued that it was entirely appropriate to have the whole range of human emotions as long as they were "timely" and manifested in terms of Confucian notions of virtue, character, and conduct. So the women then counter-argued that if this were the case, there was nothing wrong with women having strong feelings. In fact, to be able to mould these strong feelings into a productive Confucian life was a worthy task for a Confucian woman. To argue against emotions was to come too close to the unorthodox teachings of Buddhists and Daoists who struggled to get rid of their emotions altogether.

Women were also able to be educated patrons of the literary arts beyond the curriculum of the examination system because they did not have to spend the better part of their youth memorizing the classics. They did learn the classics, but not to the extent that their brothers and husbands did. They could concentrate on artistic concerns and genres.

Plate 4 *Over life-size figures of Confucius lecturing to students before a monumental bas-relief (about four storeys tall) of a Song-style landscape. The composition is located in the entry foyer of the vast new Confucian Study Center in Qufu, a clear indication of the renaissance of Confucianism in China.* Photo: Evelyn Berthrong.

4 TRANSMITTING THE DAO

While the study of history was always important for Confucians, the notion that Confucianism itself had a history that could legitimately transform over the centuries was not equally obvious to all Confucians. The reason for this was that many Confucians believed that the essence of the tradition was to revive the classical teachings of the early sages and worthies; this tendency is often called "purism" to indicate its drive to return to the early and hence "pure" teachings of the sages and worthies. The task was merely to repristinate what had always and everywhere been taught by orthodox Confucian scholars. However, other scholars, using the classical notion of being "timely," i.e. a sage who knows when to change with the changing times, countered that it was supremely Confucian to be willing to change when the historical circumstances demanded change. It was crucial to preserve the spirit but not always the letter of the tradition.

As the dynasties came and went, it became clear that there was a historical development within the Confucian tradition. The Han scholars, in preserving the records of the classical scholars and texts from the Shang and Zhou dynasties, contributed their own layer of meaning to the Confucian Way. A thousand years later, the Song revivalists also created new philosophic systems even as they argued that these new systems revived the classical learning of the Confucian past. In the historically alert age of the Qing dynasty, scholars had become even more aware that to tell the full story of the Confucian Way a scholar must pay attention to its various revivals and declines from the world of the sage kings of the distant past.

Dr. Li was honored and yet nervous about his long lecture that afternoon at the White Crane Academy. He felt privileged to have been invited by the two senior scholars at the Academy to lecture to the assembled students about the history of the Confucian Way. Dr. Li reflected that the Academy, like his own career as a scholar, was relatively new. The Academy, as was often the case for Confucian schools, had been founded only a couple of generations ago in order to encourage scholarly study and discussion. It was a commitment to the transmission and preservation of the Confucian Way. The new Qing academies and circles of correspondence between and among scholars carried on the revival of Confucian learning that began in the Song dynasties. Scholars needed places for study, conversation, reflection, and friendship. The students came to the Academy for various reasons: some indeed came because of their love of tradition and learning, but others also trooped in to prepare for the all-important local, provincial and national examinations that were, as people said, the thorny gates to success and social standing in the community. Passing the examinations was the only sure way into the imperial civil service.

There was no getting around the examinations. Ever since the Song dynasty, they had been the key to social advancement. They were open to all men, save for a few barred professions such as actors. However, it was a rare poor boy who could master the vast amount of material necessary to pass even the first of the three examinations. The first examination was at the district level. Passing that examination put at least one foot on the ladder of success. Of course, there was no hope of any official employment until a student had passed the second, provincial examination. On the positive side, as soon as a student passed the first examination, he became part of the literati class.

The second examination was given at the provincial level. It winnowed out even more aspirants for the civil service. Many great scholars never got any higher than the provincial examinations. If a student passed this level, then he might, if very lucky and well connected, be appointed to some kind of official position. However, these positions would only be at the lowest level of the civil service. But just as with the first examination, passing the provincial examination signified a deserved place among the educated elite.

Every three years the successful provincial candidates assembled in the capital to take the national examination. Those who passed were known as *jinshi* or presented scholars. The name came from the fact that they would actually be presented to the emperor. Those who were placed at the very top of the list were assured a fast-track career. Some would be appointed to the prestigious Hanlin Academy (the elite academy situated in Beijing) to learn more about the workings of the imperial government. The other successful candidates could expect various appointments in the lower rungs of the civil service.

With all of its flaws, the civil service examination system was still the best way anyone could think of to recruit talent for imperial service. It was, as the Confucians said, a career open to talent. A person's humble birth did not matter. If the young man had the talent and the support of his own and his wife's extended clan, then he could rise as high as any grand minister. Of course, political skill and luck were also part of the enduring equation.

Furthermore, not only did the young man rise, but his whole family went along with him. The ability to take care of a large family, to build a fortune, all of these things depended on success in the examinations. To be a member of the literati class from generation to generation was also the only sure way to protect the land holdings of the family. Almost all other forms of wealth were much more liable to loss through flood, fire, war, and governmental taxation or confiscation. Only land provided a secure base for the literati.

Although the government worked hard to make sure that the examinations were fair, there were all kinds of factors that helped the wealthy. The first was that it took a long, long time to pass the examinations. During the Song, when the examinations were just becoming the norm, most of the students who passed the last examination along with Master Zhu (Zhu Xi, 1130–1200) were at least thirty-five years old. That Master Zhu passed when he was only eighteen showed his genius. Many other great scholars would not pass till they were in their 40s and 50s. Considering only the family backgrounds of the young men, it might appear that many of them rose from very humble backgrounds. There was some truth in this, however, on more careful consideration it would become apparent that many of these young men were married to the daughters of already successful official families. Whenever a brilliant though poor young man was brought to the attention of an official with some "extra" daughters, it was considered a prudent action to marry the daughter to the young man and to help support his future studies. This would ensure the support of new generations of officials even if a son from the direct family line failed to pass the examinations. And last, but not least, many wealthy merchants were also more than willing to give their daughters as wives to bright young men who showed real scholarly talent and ambition. Dr. Li himself was married to a woman from an old literati family who had helped his own family support him during the long years from the first exam to the crowning glory of the national examination. The debts that these young men owed could never be repaid nor forgotten. Nor would any young official want to forget those to whom family filiality bound him in unbroken bonds of affection.

Dr. Li actually welcomed the long lecture as a chance to put his own thoughts about the history of the Confucian tradition in order. He fancied himself something of a historian of the Confucian Tao. He pondered on the many ways of approaching the study of the Confucian tradition, and he confessed to himself that he had always gravitated toward the historical approach. He believed that this was entirely appropriate because Confucius himself was vitally concerned with history. History represented the preserved records of the sage kings and their wisdom. In fact, if the traditional accounts were to be believed, Confucius was himself the author and editor of many of the classical historical works of the Confucian canon.

Confucians had always been historians. A grasp of history was essential to anyone studying for the all-important civil service examinations. The whole history of the Middle Kingdom needed to be right in the mind of the student; all the history was augmented by various approved commentaries. But more than this preparation for civil service, history was key to appropriating the tradition for oneself in service to others. This was as important to the true Confucian as success in the examinations. The reason for this was simple. All the examinations proved was that the person had a fine memory and skill at writing. No examination could look into the heart-mind and tell if the student was a genuine scholar or a mere seeker of fame and fortune.

Unless a person was born a true sage, and Dr. Li doubted that he would ever meet such a person, historical records were crucial to checking one's spiritual, moral and intellectual cultivation against the standard of the sages. The only access we have to the sages is preserved in their records. As Master Zhu said, we should read and re-read the texts of the sages and the later Confucian teachers the way we would eat a delicious meal. We should eat and read slowly and savor each morsel of the text until we have grasped its true flavor. We must make the classics part of our own being as we make food part of our bodies. We need to check behavior constantly against the writings and inspiration of the sages. All the scholarly, moral and spiritual arts of personal discipline need to be deployed in the quest for authentic personhood.

Dr. Li's own historical studies showed that there was more change than meets the eye in the history of the Middle Kingdom. China's long political and intellectual history had undergone subtle transformations. He had told the students about his evaluation of their shared tradition during the first part of the lecture that he had delivered last week. For instance, as the ruling dynasties had come and gone, the epicenter of the Chinese world had migrated from the old northern central plains to the rich lands of the Yangtze valley. No one, Dr. Li reflected, could now ignore the impact of Daoist and Buddhist thought on the systems of the Song and Ming masters of the Confucian Way. Furthermore, some of this influence was all to the good, as heretical as such an admission might sound to more conservative scholars. Who could not be instructed and amused by Zhuangzi's profound explorations of the free and easy world of spontaneous action?

The careful scholar in Dr. Li welcomed these doubts. Hadn't both Confucius and Master Zhu taught that scholarly doubt was a part of becoming an accomplished Confucian? Confucius, for instance, would not encourage the practice of certain rituals that he could not confirm as representing the real teachings of the sages. Master Zhu had gone so far as to re-edit and make additions to the *Great Learning*, one of the *Four Books*. Master Zhu, based on his own interpretation of the text, inserted a passage from the great Cheng Yi (1033–1107) concerning the proper method of study. Master Zhu had argued that the received text must have a flaw, an omission in the sense of its argument because there was no detailed explanation of the method of "examining things" in order to ascertain their principles of action and organization. Furthermore, Master Zhu and his friends had published new ritual manuals that reshaped Confucian family rituals dramatically. Dr. Li had even heard that the Koreans honored and followed Master Zhu's plan for ritual more assiduously than did the Chinese. Master Zhu's argument was that we must pay attention to both history and reason in order to understand the true teachings of the sages.

THE CLASSICAL WORLD

In the first place Dr. Li stressed that the Confucian Way was much more than a philosophic or historical teaching. While learning about the tradition was important, mere memorization of texts was useless in the long run unless there was a profound transformation of the person involved in the study of the classics of the sages. In this regard he agreed with a long line of Confucian reformers who strove to stress the spirit rather than the rote letter of the tradition. He always liked to begin with Confucius' own outline of a life dedicated to the Confucian Way.

> The Master said: "At fifteen, I set my mind upon learning. At thirty, I took my stand. At forty, I had no doubts. At fifty I knew the will of Heaven. At sixty, my ear was attuned. At seventy, I follow all the desires of my heart without breaking any rule." (Leys, 1997, p.6; 2:4)

Dr. Li had always loved this passage ever since he had memorized it himself as a young student long ago. Even then it made sense to him because it pointed a way forward from youth to mature old age and promised that this path could also be his if he dedicated himself to the task of becoming a sage.

Like the teachings of so many great thinkers, Confucius' words were deceptively simple. The first message was that learning was a lifelong process. The true task was to embark upon the process of becoming a sage. Yet Confucius himself never claimed to be a sage nor did he ever claim that he had actually met a sage in his lifetime. Nonetheless, Confucius felt secure in following his way because of the records of the past. In particular, Confucius was always moved by his reflections on the early rulers of the Zhou dynasty, namely Kings Wen and Wu and the Duke of Zhou.

Even the language was tricky here. Confucius would have thought it odd if he had been told that he was founding a new teaching. The First Teacher, one of the favorite titles for Confucius, believed that he was not creating something new. Rather, Confucius believed that he was reviving the authentic teachings of the early sages. Debate has raged ever since about what Confucius meant by his statement about not creating but rather transmitting the teachings of the ancient sages. Confucius loved tradition because it was the repository of the deeds and words of sagely rulers and ministers. It was the mirror of proper conduct that we must hold up when we ask, are we acting in a moral, humane way?

Dr. Li understood Confucius' point about wanting to transmit the teaching of the first sages. However, Dr. Li also realized that in seeking to teach these primordial truths to a wider circle than ever before, Confucius had altered irrevocably the history of the Confucian Way. For instance, when Confucius suggested that *ren* or humanity (humaneness) was to be cultivated as the virtue of a truly civilized person, this expanded the range of the concept for all time. The First Teacher had taught young men from all walks and stations in life for whom *ren* was a form of *noblesse oblige*, that humaneness was a universal personal virtue open to all people regardless of their social standing. In fact, one of the most exciting things that Confucius ever did was to open up the teaching of "this culture of ours" to everyone who was interested.

In later times, especially after the arrival of Buddhism in China during the Han dynasty (*c.* 200 B.C.E.–200 C.E.), it was easier to see what was unique about the teachings of the Confucian scholars. Dr. Li did have to admit that it was something of a problem to explain the precise terminology and concepts he used to talk about the development of the Confucian Way as it evolved over time. For example, ever since the Song and Ming, people discussed the Way of Confucius and Mencius as the mainline of the tradition. But what about all the other great masters such as Xunzi, the third of the great classical Zhou masters, or Han Yü (768–824) in the Tang? Xunzi was excluded from this definition of the Way because of his arguments with Mencius about human nature. Yet Dr. Li admitted, at least to himself, that he held Xunzi in high regard because of his defense of ritual and because of his keen mind and analytic abilities. It struck Dr. Li that the tradition needed Xunzi's profound contribution as much as it revered Mencius' reflections on the ultimate goodness of the human mind-heart.

The question was even more pressing for Dr. Li, after some recent conversations with the strange "Western Scholars," as the Jesuit missionaries were affectionately known by their Chinese friends, about the nature of the Confucian Way. They asked all kinds of questions that he had never thought about before. The questions of these learned missionaries were based, Dr. Li had to admit, on solid Confucian scholarship. The Jesuits argued that the Confucian Way had begun with a reverence for *tian* (heaven), which the Jesuit fathers interpreted as the same reality as their Western Christian God. As Dr. Li pondered the question he reread Master Zhu's conversations about this religious interpretation with his students and discovered that even Master Zhu was willing to acknowledge that you could read some of the most ancient canonical references to *tian* as God.

Notwithstanding the plausibility of this line of exegesis, Dr. Li found it disturbing and off-centered. If you accepted the Jesuit reading as apt, then wouldn't this lower the Confucian tradition to the level of the other popular, and from Dr. Li's perspective, superstitious religions of the common people? Although Dr. Li himself recognized a religious dimension, a spirituality if you like, to the tradition, this was not the heart of the Confucian Way. Whereas the Taoists explored the question of God, god and gods from within the pan-Chinese worldview, the Confucians did not. And of course, the Buddhists resolutely rejected any notion of divinity whatsoever.

The heart of the tradition was in what Confucius called "one thread" that went throughout all of his teachings.

> The Master said, "Shen, my doctrine has one single thread running through it." Master Zeng Shen replied" "Indeed."
> The Master left. The other disciples asked: "What did he mean?" Master Zeng said: "The doctrine of the Master is: Loyalty and reciprocity, and that's all." (Leys, 1997, p.17; 4:15).

Other ways to phrase being loyal was to be faithful and constant in pushing yourself to the utmost effort; to put oneself in another's place was reciprocity or forgiveness. It was the "that's all" that always gave Dr. Li pause for reflection.

Of course, later scholars unanimously agreed that Confucius was here giving one of his typical illustrations of the virtue of *ren* or humanity. Undoubtedly this is the virtue of virtue for Confucians. "The Master said: Seeking to achieve humanity leaves no room for evil." (Leys 1997, p.15; 4:4). What Dr. Li loved about pondering these cryptic statements of Confucius was that they pointed him in two directions. This virtue of *ren* was the essence of the Way itself. If you could get it for yourself in service to others, you would find peace. As Confucius put it, "In the morning hear the Way; in the evening die content" (Leys 1997, p.16; 4:8). This was the path of proper conduct among other people; it was the resolute spirit of steadfast humaneness towards all people. Of course, the First Teacher was not always grim; there were many passages wherein he spoke of the pure joy of finding the proper way among all other possible ways.

There was a wonderful rhythm to the cultivation and practice of *ren*/humaneness, rather like the oscillations of the primordial forces of yin and yang. The first movement was always focused on the cultivation of the self in order better to understand human nature and the mind-heart. But that moment of pure personal self-cultivation and movement towards the center of the self then always swung outwards towards service to family and other people. Only a petty, perverse person kept humanity (*ren*) without sharing it with others. The second movement was *shu* as a kind of empowered altruism. You must persevere in your own authenticity as an ethical person in order to be of any real use to other persons. And to extend this authentic personhood, you had to have the ability to put yourself in the place of others, i.e. a profound and informed empathy.

What was the message of the sages across time? The message was simple at one level. Probably his favorite definition was to get the Way for oneself in service to others. This demanded the cultivation of empathy in the self, a recognition of humaneness and justice and a willingness to play a number of roles in private and public life. In short, it was a mandate to bring order to the self, family, and society. However, this was all really connected in the sense that there was no self without the family and society and the family and society, in turn, needed the honest and forthright services of men of independent moral and intellectual characters.

Dr. Li wanted to stress the large sweep of the development and transformation of the Confucian Way. There were really five major movements in the music of the Way. The first was the classical period that began with Confucius' initial definitions of the Way itself. This was followed by the work of the second sage, Mencius, and concluded with the life of Xunzi. Although Xunzi was not highly regarded by Confucians after the Song dynasty because of his quarrel with Mencius about human nature, Dr. Li very much appreciated the contribution of Xunzi to the defense of the Way against other philosophers of Warring States China. His emphasis on clear thinking and the role of ritual in the constitution of civilization were major contributions to the development of the Confucian Way.

Of course, Confucius never thought that he was "inventing" a new philosophic system. In fact, all the Master ever claimed for himself was that he had never met anyone who loved learning more than he did. Confucius believed that he lived in dangerous times when the founding virtues of the great Kings Wen and Wu and the Duke of Zhou were losing their power. Confucius sought to reverse this decline in the culture of his day by reminding scholars that this culture was their birthright. Although Dr. Li doubted that Confucius realized what he was doing, he became the first private teacher. If he could not find a prince to work with him in restoring the pristine culture of the early Zhou, he could at least pass this wisdom along to his disciples.

Confucius looked back not only to the founders of the Zhou, but to the great culture heroes of the even more remote past. But they were not remote to Confucius. He loved to study them and to travel from state to state seeking records of the ancient sages and worthies. There was even a story told about an interview Master Kong had with Laozi. This Laozi was an archivist in charge of records and Kong wanted to review them. Of course, the later Daoists used this story to prove that their teacher, Laozi, was, in fact, the teacher of Master Kong. This meant that, following the virtue of deference, Confucians really ought to defer to Daoists. Needless to say, this was not the lesson that the Confucians drew from the encounter.

Although Confucius never outlined or explained in great detail his philosophy, later masters such as Mencius and even Xunzi rose to the defense of the master. They pointed out that Confucius, in his role as a great teacher, was rescuing the learning of the sages and worthies for future generations. It was because of people like Confucius that we remember the heroic deeds of the great sage emperors such as Yao and Shun. It was the task of all Confucians to take the enduring principles taught by the ancient sages and apply them to their own day.

On the whole, Confucius loved the old rituals, stories, and poetry. However, Confucius understood that we were long removed from the great days of the early sage kings. In fact, he made it clear that he followed his own ruling house, the Zhou, in teaching proper ritual. However, even if the specifics of a ritual may change because of time and condition, the essential meaning of the rituals should never be abandoned. These virtues were given to human beings by heaven itself, engraved, as it were, on the mind-hearts of the living. It was our task to revere and revive these virtues in order to create a civilized world.

Along with the work of the three great masters of the classical period, there were many other important canonical works composed or edited during the period between Confucius, Mencius, and the death of Xunzi. According to the received tradition, Confucius collected and edited many of these poetic, ritual, and historical texts. All of these texts continued to be important for Confucians, though some had become more important than others. For instance, works such as *The Classic of Filial Piety*, the *Great Learning*, and the *Doctrine of the Mean* had taken on independent lives of their own. Other classics, such as *The Classic of Changes*, continued to exert influences in an uninterrupted fashion from century to century.

Recently Dr. Li had re-read the works of Xunzi. No one doubted Xunzi's brilliance. It was his lack of commonsense in picking a quarrel with Mencius that had tarnished his reputation ever since Mencius was declared to be the second sage by the Song philosophers. The issue was Xunzi's teaching that human nature was evil whereas Mencius had taught that human nature was good. This was a deep philosophic puzzle. If human nature is what makes us what we are, and if it is evil, then where can we find the solid virtues we need to make us fully human? Mencius had defended the Confucian Way against the other teachers of the Warring States period by maintaining that we must find these virtues right in our mind-heart and human nature. Of course, Mencius was quite clear that we must cultivate these incipient virtues, what he called the four sprouts or seeds of virtue, arduously lest they wither and die for lack of attention.

Dr. Li had now been a city magistrate for long enough to harbor some sympathy for Xunzi's counter teaching that human nature was evil. There was something of an exasperated tone in Xunzi one suspected. Mencius, even though he always used all kinds of horticultural metaphors, had made it too easy. All we had to do was to look within our mind-hearts, to discover our human nature, and to water the seeds until we had our garden of virtue. Xunzi demurred; he held that it was only through the education of ritual that we could hope to become good. We could not merely rely on the examination of our unaided and untutored mind-hearts. What was decent about any person was the artifice of ritual. When you understood that Xunzi was striving for the same noble end as Mencius, you could see why no one denied that he was a Confucian. Some bold scholars in the Qing went so far as to argue that Confucianism would never be a realistic, sophisticated philosophy until and unless it made a place again for Xunzi among the classics of the Confucian tradition.

The main thrust of all of the work of the great classical masters was to reflect on the cultivation of virtue, human nature, and the reformation of the social order. If Dr. Li had known about them, he would have likened the work of these early masters to the work of thinkers such as Socrates, Plato, and Aristotle. The early Confucians discussed many things, even including topics such as epistemology and logic, but all of their thoughts were focused on the cultivation of the self and the reconstruction of society. They believed that the former sages, represented by Kings Wen, Wu, and the Duke of Zhou, provided the necessary models for human conduct.

THE ORDERLY HAN

The second period was the work of the Confucians of the Han dynasty. They were not as lionized as the founders of the tradition, but their role was still a vital one. One of the most important things that they did was to recover as many classics and texts as they could salvage from the great wars that had led to the founding of the Qin and subsequently the Han dynasties. The ferocity of these great wars of consolidation had caused the loss of many priceless works. The Qin, to its eternal discredit, had followed the advice of its Legalist ministers and had tried to eliminate almost all the philosophic schools of the early period. They were unfortunately successful in their effort to stamp out schools beyond their own Legalist tradition (with some exceptions such as works on medicine and farming).

What books the Qin authorities had not confiscated and banned were also at risk during the civil wars that ended the life of the unlamented reign of the Qin emperors. It was a bibliographic catastrophe of the first magnitude. One of the things that the scholars of the Han set off to do was to try to find all the texts they could. They were highly successful in many cases. Along with collecting the texts, the Han erudites began to collate and edit them. In some cases they would only have parts of a text and it was their task to try to put the various pieces back together again. They were so skillful at their work that their texts have remained the received texts of the tradition from their time on. The Confucian Way owes a huge debt to the scholars of the Han for lovingly preserving and editing the whole pre-Han corpus.

The Han Confucians also added their own commentaries to the classics. Many times their appended commentaries became classics in their own right. Later scholars learned to read the early works through the eyes of the Han thinkers, who had actually added some interesting new ways of reading the classics. For instance, they were much more fascinated by cosmological and metaphysical speculations than had been Confucius, Mencius, or Xunzi.

The Han scholars added the cosmological dimension of Chinese thought to the Confucian Way. In doing so they believed that they were simply clarifying the Way and not modifying it. Later scholars would not always agree, but the addition of cosmological theories to Confucian thought did expand the range of the traditions considerably. For instance, prior to the Han dynasty, Confucians had not shown very much interest in the theories about the role of yin-yang and the Five Phases in the creation of the world. The early Confucians had simply either ignored this kind of cosmology or assumed much of it as the basis of their thought. They did not feel any need to discuss it.

The Han scholars, such as Dong Zhongshu, were fascinated by theories about the five phases, *qi*, and the unceasing interaction of yin and yang. They linked these cosmological speculations to political theory in order to generate elaborate philosophies of history. From their point of view they were simply explicating the cosmos more fully. The reason for this elaboration of the tradition was always to be in service to the perennial Confucian concerns for personal and social ethics. This fusion of natural philosophy and personal and social ethics remained a gift of the Han scholars to the rest of the history of Confucianism.

Although the history of Confucianism was written as if there were only the classical masters and the great Song revival, the Confucian debt to the Han was immeasurable. For instance, it was the Han scholars who codified the teachings on virtue. Whenever Confucians talked about the virtues, they always mentioned five cardinal virtues – at least after the Han. Of course, the Confucians had always recognized these five virtues, but it was the genius of the Han scholars to weave the various teachings about virtue together into a coherent whole. The Han provided the enduring list of five human virtues.

The five virtues, each linked to a family or social relation, are:

Ren: humaneness; without humaneness, there would be no virtue. *Ren* was the virtue of humaneness between parents and children.

I: righteousness or the sense of justice. This was the virtue of respect and deference between ruler and minister.

Li: ritual or civility; the ability to act in a proper fashion. The mutual respect and balance between husband and wife.

Zhi: wisdom, knowledge, and discernment. The virtue of the affection between older and younger siblings.

Xin: faithfulness in thought, word, and deed. The virtue of friendship and reciprocity.

The Han scholars here demonstrated their ability to synthesize, rationally, the teachings of the Zhou masters. By linking the five virtues to the five cosmic phases the Han scholars created a system of thought that was a natural extension of the pan-Chinese cultural sensibilities for all time. Every Confucian girl and boy would take in the five virtues with their mother's milk. Moreover, the virtue of faithfulness between friends always made the system an open one. While it was true that most of the virtues were based on family relationships or relationships of authority, the value of friendship reached out across all possible barriers in trust and genuine solidarity.

Dr. Li had always felt a special affinity with the virtue of faithfulness and its link to friendship. Friendship was a key element in the life of Confucian scholars. Of course, every person had the primordial connections given by birth and family. But beyond the family there was the circle of friends. Confucius himself had recommended friends and colleagues as teachers. The First Master had taught that we can learn from any virtuous and intelligent person that we stumble across during the journey of our lives. Moreover, we must be careful in picking our circle of friends. They will be our companions during the task of self-cultivation. Our friends can correct us when we make mistakes, just as we have a duty to remonstrate with them when we see them falling into error or evil ways. And, beyond all of this, they provide us with the simple pleasures of comradeship along the way.

BUDDHIST INTERRUPTIONS

However, great philosophic periods, just like the dynasties themselves, decline. After the glory of the classical period and its restoration under the Han, there was the interregnum of Daoism and Buddhism. Just as the Han dynasty entered its terminal decline, the religion of the Buddha entered China at the end of the first century. It arrived hardly noticed but soon became a dominant religious, intellectual, and social force in Chinese life. Although the Confucian Way did not disappear, it did decline in general importance. From the second to the ninth centuries many of the best minds of China either became Buddhists or were fascinated by the Buddha's teaching. And where the Buddhists did not dominate between the long period of time between the fall of the Han to the rise of the Song, religious Daoists abounded. Even though Buddhism had gone into decline after the Song dynasty, it was still a strong force in

Chinese society. For instance, it was a religion of choice for many women. Dr. Li's own mother was a patron of her local Buddhist monastery.

The Confucian world had never encountered another high culture prior to the arrival of Buddhism. All the previous contacts had been with barbarians; and for the most part they were difficult and military in nature. From time to time after the fall of the Han till the revival of the glorious Tang dynasty in the seventh century, northern and central Asian barbarian groups had even conquered parts of North China, though they were never able to subdue the whole country. Many of these tribal confederations and mixed sino-barbarian dynasties became great patrons of the Buddhist culture. If truth be told, the founding house of the Tang dynasty itself was of mixed Chinese and barbarian background. Perhaps that was one reason that the Tang dynasty was so expansive and open to the outside world. The Tang was a great empire and welcomed new ideas, new poetry, and even new wines and food from the outside world. There was a love of life that was so fresh and expansive about all things Tang.

Dr. Li was not the kind of Confucian who despised Buddhism. He was a good friend with a learned local Buddhist abbot – who was a retired official with impeccable literati credentials. He respected the learning and religious piety of his Buddhist friend even if he disagreed on major philosophic and social points. For instance, Buddhism had a major place for celibate monastic orders for both men and women. Such a form of social organization had been unknown in China before Buddhism. Confucians believed that the family was the matrix of the person; Buddhists left the family. Confucians believed that all the human emotions were part of human nature even if they had to be vigorously cultivated and sometimes regulated; the Buddhists taught about nirvana, a state of religious awakening beyond even perfected human nature, much less the more mundane human passions of family and state.

Nonetheless, Dr. Li recognized that the Buddhist challenge had forced the great Confucian reformers of the Song dynasty to add profound new philosophic dimensions to the classical ethical vision and cosmology of the Confucian Way. The Buddhists demanded the formation of a Confucian moral metaphysics designed to counter the seductive teachings of the Buddha's *dharma*. If the Buddhists defended the emptiness of nirvana as the ultimate reality, it was incumbent on the Confucians to provide a counter-argument for the reality and validity of the world.

SONG REVIVALS

If the classical age of Confucius, Mencius and Xunzi was the first golden age of the Confucian Way, the great revival of the Song dynasty was the second greatest flowering of the tradition. The names of the Song literati tripped from the tongue like a catalog of immortals. The revival really began with a call from the throne for proposals for reforming the institutions of Song China. Scholars such as Fan Zhongyan (989–1052) responded to the appeal with a set of proposals for reform that went beyond merely tinkering with the formal structures of government. These reforms sought to renovate Chinese society from top to bottom. Moreover, these reforms were based squarely in a sense of Confucian revival. The only way for a truly successful reform was an intellectual revolution based on Confucian principles.

There was a second wave of reforms presented in the next generation and forever linked to the name of Wang Anshi (prime minister in the 1060s). The reforms that Wang presented to the throne became known as the New Policies, and they touched on every aspect of Chinese life from local education to national fiscal policy. But there was more to Wang's appeal. Wang buttressed his reforms with a new interpretation of the classical tradition. Wang agreed with Fan that reform needed to be supported by a renewed vision of the Confucian Way. Good government must be based on the appointment of good men as ministers. And good ministers must have a proper Confucian education. Governmental policy and self-cultivation must be fused into a seamless whole. Wang's New Policies were utopian; and all utopias are problematic.

People either loved or hated Wang Anshi and his reforms. Scholars had debated them endlessly. In the end, the reforms mostly failed but, the controversies that swirled around the New Policies produced reactions that reverberated down through the ages. A group of scholars opposed to Wang's reforms and philosophy arose and became known as the Masters of the Northern Song. As a group they were less influential as political leaders but were famous as philosophers. In fact, Dr. Li noted, the monumental official history of the Song dynasty even gave them their own section separate from that devoted to other Confucian scholars. These remarkable men were known to history as *Daoxue* or the School of the Way.

Many other Confucian scholars scoffed at the pretensions of this group of philosophers. What gave them the right to call themselves guardians of the true Confucian Way? Such attacks did not deter the Northern Song masters from their appointed tasks. They perceived their struggle with Wang Anshi as a struggle for the mind-heart of China. Because Wang professed to be a Confucian they needed to provide a Confucian critique of his reforms and philosophy. Although they shared much of Wang's political and social passions, they vehemently disagreed with the specifics of his readings of the classics. From their point of view, to begin the process of cosmic reform with a mistaken philosophic and moral agenda could only lead to disaster for the Confucian Way and the Chinese empire in the end.

Truly the names of Shao Yong, Zhou Dunyi, Zhang Zai, the brothers Cheng Hao and Cheng Yi were landmarks in the history of Confucianism. Collectively they shaped the future direction of the Confucian Way because of their varied philosophic contributions. One of their collective presuppositions was that real reform must be based on personal reform; furthermore, personal reform could only rest on secure philosophic foundations. Confucians must return to the cultivation of the mind-heart in a proper fashion. They devised ways to carry out this cultivation based on study and meditation. In forming their new Song synthesis they also produced a new and comprehensive vision of the Confucian Way. What was unique was that the moral and cosmological concerns of the Zhou, Han, and Tang dynasties were now fused with a comprehensive and systematic philosophic vision. Taken together the Northern and Southern Song revivalists engendered a new speculative Confucian worldview.

Among the Northern Song revivalists, Shao Yong (1011–77) was the most difficult to define for a number of reasons. First, his thought lurked at the farthest reaches of the emerging School of the Way sense of orthodoxy. For instance, Shao was fascinated by numerology and its application to life and history. He was also inordinately interested in epistemological questions, though these studies were deeply appreciated by some later Confucian scholars. Second, Shao did not follow the normal career path expected of someone of his brilliance. He never sat for the examinations and therefore never entered the civil service. Rather, Shao was known as the hermit of Luoyang.

Third, when the great Zhu Xi established the history of the orthodox Way, he refused to include Shao Yong in the canonical list of Northern Song masters. Although Shao was probably the first of this stalwart group to write philosophy, Zhu always recognized Zhou Dunyi as the first of the Northern Song masters. Zhu argued that while Shao was a Confucian,

Shao's whole edifice of speculative thought was too close to heterodox forms of Daoist numerology. For instance, Shao had the reputation of having an arcane ability to tell the future. All of this struck Master Zhu as a step too far for an orthodox Confucian master. None of this, however, ever stopped later Confucian scholars, including Master Zhu, from reading and citing the impressive legacy of Shao. The most important element in Shao's work was an extended meditation on the *Book of Changes*.

The acknowledged founder of the School of the Way was Zhou Dunyi, and there was little doubt that he deserved the title. Although Zhou only wrote two short texts, his works had a tremendous impact on the shape of Confucian thought. The most dramatic example was the justly famous *Diagram of the Supreme Ultimate*. This was a very short work, but it served as a manifesto for the philosophic and cosmological themes of the School of the Way. It provided, albeit in a highly schematic fashion, a figurative outline of the process of the Dao from the Confucian point of view. It was also enigmatic enough to provide ample room for all kinds of plausible interpretations of what Master Zhou meant when he stated at the very beginning, "The Supreme Ultimate and the Non-Ultimate." Dr. Li noted that it was as difficult to say precisely what Master Zhou had in mind in his short sentence as it was to figure out the opening of Laozi's *Daodejing*.

Regardless of how the opening sentence should be read, it provided a warrant for a new Confucian cosmological vision of reality. Moreover, in Master Zhou's other works he demonstrated how a new cosmological scheme ought to be connected to traditional Confucian moral concerns. What was really novel was that ethics could be read as a profound examination of ultimate cosmological values. The classical Confucian values were interpreted as not only foundational for social life, but emblematic for all reality as such. Master Zhou's world was a social and realistic place when compared to the Confucian understanding of the alternative Daoist and Buddhist readings of reality. The Confucians claimed that they based their thought on solid reality as opposed to Buddhist doctrines of emptiness and the Daoist teachings of non-being. Of course, Dr. Li's Daoist and Buddhist friends objected strenuously that this was neither a charitable nor accurate interpretation of what they really meant by emptiness and non-being. Nonetheless, Master Zhou and the School of the Way stoutly defended the reality of common human experience.

The second of the orthodox Northern Song masters was Zhang Zai.

He was a friend of Master Zhou and the uncle of the precocious Cheng brothers. Zhang's name had been inextricably linked to the notion of *qi*. Zhang defended the notion that vital force or matter-energy was the fundamental or primordial bedrock of all reality. What was, or is, or will be, is *qi*. The world exists because of the ceaseless generativity of vital force.

Dr. Li found it important to teach his students what Zhang meant by *qi*. *Qi* was so fundamental to all forms of Chinese thought that people always assumed they knew what it meant. Was it a thing? Clearly yes. Was it a spirit or foundation of the movement of the mind-heart? Again, clearly yes. But vital force was not without form or process. The concreteness of things was a mark of how vital force manifested itself in the world. Moreover, and always important for a Confucian thinker, vital force also was driving energy for ethical actions. Proper rituals and actions were just as "concrete" in terms of the configuration of vital force as any stone on the street.

Along with being the philosopher of vital force par excellence, Zhang Zai also stressed the role of ethical self-cultivation. Zhang's favorite ethical theme was the notion of *cheng* as self-realization. Zhang used self-realization as a way to describe what the desired outcome for self-cultivation ultimately entailed. Zhang stressed that a Confucian must realize the five virtues and that the state of realizing these virtues was to be found in self-realization. Zhang chose as his canonical source for *cheng*-theory the *Doctrine of the Mean*. According to Zhang, if a person could realize their full human potential through proper self-cultivation, then a person could become self-actualized and become, as the classical text promised, a co-creator of the world along with heaven and earth.

Zhang's sense of self-cultivation provided him with a profound respect for all the living creatures of the earth. He inscribed a famous short essay known as the *Western Inscription* over the west window of his study that expressed his deepest spiritual feelings about the world. Although the Confucian Way was not a religion in the sense of Buddhism or popular Daoism, nor like the new Western religion of Christianity, there was a tremendous spiritual vision within the tradition as expressed by Zhang in the *Western Inscription*.

The Cheng brothers were the most famous fraternal pair in the history of Chinese thought. The older brother, Cheng Hao, was one of the most appealing figures of the whole Song revival. Along with being a first-rate intellectual, he was, by all accounts, a wonderfully humane and sincere man. All counted themselves lucky to be his friend. The most important teaching of both Cheng Hao and Cheng Yi was the doctrine of principle. The notion of principle pervaded all of their writings and provided the formal contrast to Zhang Zai's concept of vital force.

In short, the Chengs argued that everything that is has a special form. There is an ultimate form for all reality and we call that the Supreme Ultimate, here following the lead of Zhou Dunyi. But each and every thing, in order to be what it is when compared and contrasted to all other things, has its own form. This is a philosophic rule that runs from Heaven to the most mundane things of the world. The term *li* originally meant the patterns in a piece of jade. This struck the Cheng brothers as a profound metaphorical insight into the nature of things. While vital energy is a basis for all that is, for anything to be this thing rather than something else, it needed its own principle or pattern of order. This is what *li* provided for the Cheng brothers. Principle became the normative element not only for concrete things but also for the prime ethical virtues.

This point about order, pattern, and principle is a key notion. For the Chengs, a proper ethical action or ritual was just as definite a thing as a book or chair. Both the ethical action and the chair had their formal principle. The principal of a chair was to hold people when sitting. If it did so, preferably with some comfort, then it fulfilled its form as a chair. If the chair fell apart or unceremoniously dumped its occupant on the floor, then it did not merit the name of a chair and failed to fulfil its principle. If a friend was not faithful to a friend, then the pattern or form of faithfulness was violated. Merely knowing what a virtue was and failing to embody the virtue meant that a person had forsaken the principle of the virtue. In many respects the Chengs' notion of principle linked philosophically to Confucius' concern for the rectification of names. What the Chengs accomplished was an explanation of how we would know when a name was actually rectified.

The Chengs made the point that principle was one and its manifestations were many. This meant that all principles were linked through the Supreme Ultimate, which manifested itself in the specific principles of each thing or person. However, the unity of principle was moral or normative. There was for each and every principle a better or worse way for it to be realized. The focus was, of course, on the task of becoming fully human. The practice of realization found expression in moral conduct. The ultimate norms were, therefore, moral in character in the sense that they expressed fineness or coarseness, and so forth. Principle truly found expression in the moral cultivation of the person and the person's role in the larger world.

Next in line of the great Song thinkers was the Southern Song scholar Zhu Xi. Although he never studied with the Northern Song masters, he did study with their disciples and students and imbibed their insights. He created the grand synthesis of Song learning that dominated Confucian studies from that time on. Although he died under a cloud of accusations about the appropriateness of his teachings, in a very short while his work was formally accepted as the norm for the civil service examinations by the Mongol Yuan dynasty in 1313. Zhu's dominance, as the voice of Song orthodoxy, continued with the foundation of the Chinese Ming dynasty and was continued by the Qing after their conquest of China in 1644.

Master Zhu managed to find a place for all the major themes of his beloved Northern Song masters. He achieved this integration by focusing his attention on two aspects of the moral philosophy of the Southern Song. In the first place he developed a theory about the nature and cultivation of the human mind-heart. Zhu argued that the mind-heart was the most refined form of vital force for the human person and contained both the emotions generated from the motions of the vital force and the intellectual ability to perceive principle or the formal ordering patterns of things and events. Moreover, the mind-heart contained the seeds of moral sentiment as Mencius had taught so long ago. The mind-heart, according to Master Zhu, and in this he followed Zhang Zai, united the principle of human nature as endowed by heaven with the emotions generated by the ceaseless flux of vital force.

Master Zhu believed that the mind-heart could pay the proper deference due both sides of a living person through a regimen of intense education and self-cultivation. Here too Master Zhu relied on the classical tradition that taught that although the moral sentiments were a gift of heaven to each human being, their maturation and even manifestation depended on human effort. As Master Zhu, and Dr. Li as well, loved to remind his students, the mind-heart of the Dao was precarious in nature and the mind-heart of uncultivated persons was prone to wander beyond the realms of reason and proper conduct. The only way for the all too human and passionate hearts of persons to conform to the principles of heaven was for each person to practice self-cultivation in order to achieve the actualization of true humanity.

In the second place, Master Zhu linked his interpretation of the human mind-heart to a theory of the unity of vital force and principle that relied on the integration of the insights of Zhang Zai and the Cheng brothers. Master Zhu's philosophic innovation was to abstract from his theory of human nature the theory that principle and vital energy were everywhere and always conjoined in the manifestation of any thing or event. They were held together by the agency of the Supreme Ultimate as the locus or norm needed to adjudicate the harmony of principle and vital force. Each thing or event fused these two elements into a whole. By linking principle and vital force by means of a prototype of moral achievement, namely the Supreme Ultimate, Master Zhu was able to do justice to the metaphysical and the moral dimensions of the Confucian project.

Although Master Zhu was most famous for his ability to synthesize the contributions of the Northern Song philosophers, his theory was actually even more subtle than merely balancing the dyads of yin and yang, principle and vital force, the human mind-heart and Dao mind-'heart. Zhu showed how these primordial contrasting pairs could be unified in practice and theory. The complexity of his thought was both what bothered his critics and the source of inspiration to his disciples.

Master Zhu had a way of showing how the dyads, say of human nature, the emotions, and the mind-heart functioned together in bringing order and harmony to human life. The inherited dyads of the classical tradition became a triadic portrait of the formal, dynamic, and unifying traits of anything whatsoever. For instance, nowhere was this tripartite discourse more evident than in the way Master Zhu demonstrated the philosophic structure of the relationships of human nature, the emotions, and the mind-heart. This was a perfect example, according to Zhu, of the enduring pattern of principle, vital force, and actualization in the generative world of the Way. As the Appendix of *The Classic of Changes* taught, the way, or principle as Zhu would take it, was itself constant production and reproduction without cessation.

A systematic outline of the relationship of the various elements looks like this:

- Human nature is principle: human nature as principle provides the formal patterns of order and regulation of things and events.
- The emotions are vital force: vital force provides the dynamic trait of ceaseless production and reproduction.
- The mind-heart unifies principle and vital force: the mind-heart actualizes (the virtue of *cheng* as the full expression of *ren*) principle and

vital force in full and inclusive humanity. This is also expressed as the Supreme Ultimate.

• The harmony, *ho*, of the mind-heart as it interacts with other persons amid the reciprocal, *pao*, generativity of the Dao.

This was a good outline of Master Zhu's philosophic vision, with the addition of the notion of harmony. We have added *ho* or harmony because of the axiological (theory of values) nature of Zhu's thought – as with Aristotle there is always an end for any action, including ethical conduct. But there is still another step to be taken; after there is a realization of humaneness, this must be expressed both to other people and as ongoing behavior directed into the future. Therefore, to stop with the rather formal tripartite alternation of form – dynamic, and unification and the harmony of achieved and anticipated new actions – misses one of the most important elements of his thought. None of the speculative elements would make any sense or would have any value unless they were in service of something living and virtue. There was a perfectionist strain in Zhu's thought. Zhu was always concerned with ethical self-cultivation. Zhu believed that good theory was only good in the sense that it assisted in the perfection of human life. And the perfection of human life was ultimately ethical and social in nature.

Along with his outline of the moral and metaphysical nature of human beings, Master Zhu also provided a curriculum for the realization of human nature. The most famous result was the grouping of four works taken from the thirteen Confucian classics and calling them the *Four Books*. They were the *Great Learning*, the *Analects*, the *Mencius*, and the *Doctrine of the Mean*. Master Zhu added his own authoritative commentary to these works and even radically edited and emended the *Great Learning*. The Four Books, according to Master Zhu, then became the point of entry into the study of the Confucian classics and other important philosophic, poetic, and historical works. Along with his good friend Lü Zuqian, Master Zhu also compiled a collection of the writings of the Northern Song Masters, *Reflections on Things at Hand*, which served as an introduction to the Four Books and to the thought of the School of the Way as interpreted by Master Zhu.

Master Zhu did not stop with writing commentaries and philosophic works. He was vitally concerned with the reformation and spread of proper ritual conduct. To this end he began the composition of a major work entitled *Master Zhu's Family Rituals*. The new manual of ritual theory and practice attempted to spell out in comprehensible detail the various rituals necessary for Confucian family life. It covered everything from marriage to burial. It too became a guide for conduct for generations of Chinese literati families.

Of course, not everyone appreciated Master Zhu's massive synthesis of Song Confucian thought and practice. One of the main criticisms centered on the proper mode of study necessary to realize Confucian virtues. Master Zhu's favorite expression was taken from the *Great Learning* where it was urged that we all must examine things in order to exhaust or understand their principles. Master Zhu took the admonition to examine things very seriously. While he was mostly concerned with the study of the Confucian classics, he also encouraged his students to read material from other Chinese schools and to pay attention to the world around them. Although not a professional naturalist, he took a keen interest in the best scientific thought of his day.

CONTINUING IN THE MING AND QING

Master Zhu's critics argued that his theory of the examination of things externalized the study of principle. They countered, against all the *lixue*, that the proper form of Confucian self-cultivation must begin with the rectification of the mind-heart before it became hopelessly lost in the minutiae of the mundane world. The debate about the proper way to travel the path of the Confucian Way continued to rage through the whole Ming period into the Qing dynasty.

One of the main bones of contention was the inward turning direction of Ming thought, though it was unlikely that the scholars would have conceived of their work in this way. Nonetheless, the trajectory of scholarly concern focused more and more on the cultivation of the mind-heart. The more academic and outward looking stance of Zhu Xi was challenged by the great Wang Yangming (1472–1529). Wang firmly believed that Master Zhu sought for the fundamental mind-heart in the wrong direction. Zhu was too interested in the external study of the world and of texts. The real task of the scholar was to cultivate the mind-heart.

Wang Yangming's challenge was based on the most dramatic tale of Confucian enlightenment. Wang had been whipped in front of the whole court and then banished from the capital to the far south because of his support of a friend against one of the most powerful eunuchs then in favor with the emperor. Wang was in despair about his career, but even more so because he was unsure about the moral foundations of his action. In his exile Wang recorded that, as he was meditating in front of a stone coffin reflecting on ultimate questions of life and death, suddenly the question of the mind-heart and the examination of things became clear. Wang realized that his own human nature was sufficient for the task of achieving sagehood; he had been looking for the principle of things in the outside world whereas what he needed to do was to search in his own mind-heart.

After his realization of the profound epistemological implications of his sudden insight, Wang devoted the rest of his philosophic career to teaching students how to cultivate the self properly. He taught that the mind-heart was indeed principle. You could not find principle in things outside of the mind-heart. Wang believed that he had found the key to Mencius' teaching about finding the seeds of morality within our own human nature through the cultivation of the mind-heart. He also taught how his new doctrine joined action and thought without any hint of separation. According to Wang, theory and practice must always be conjoined; if you claim to understand the principle of filial piety, then this is only a viable claim if and only if you are actually filial to your parents. He instructed his students that knowledge was the inception of action and that action completed knowledge. Out of all this reflection on the unity of theory and action came Wang's famous demand for the extending of the basic goodness of each and every person.

What was curious about Wang Yangming's stance was that he was probably the most "active" of all the Neo-Confucians. He was a great general; he was also the finest poet of the whole group. Moreover, Wang argued that his insights into the fundamental mind led not to passive quietism, but to more action in the world. Wang Yangming struggled against the potential functional dualism he thought lurked in Master Zhu's system. In order to do so he often phrased his teachings in gnomic formulations that struck other Confucians as teachings perilously close to Chan Buddhism. None of this mattered to Wang. If he could help his students achieve the fundamental good mind, and to carry out the Confucian project in action, then he was satisfied. Moreover, like Confucius before him, Wang was willing to accept students from all walks of life and not just from the literati class. It was, as his students would say, as if the streets were filled with sages.

The later students of Wang Yangming took his teachings to heart and fanned out to teach as widely as possible. Some, from the famous or infamous Taizhou school, did attempt to find those sages in the streets by preaching Wang's message to the broad mass of people. Because of the Taizhou school's emphasis on ordinary life, they were famous for valorizing the emotions much more than other Confucians. Because of this emphasis, many educated women followed their philosophic lead. Dr. Li, introduced to their poetry by Mrs. Li, read with appreciation the fine poetry of these educated Ming ladies.

The Taizhou radicals and the educated women of the late Ming made a valid argument. Wang Yangming had proved that we can only recover principle within our mind-hearts. Moreover, when we examine our mind-hearts, we find them filled with emotions. Confucians, as opposed to the Daoists and Buddhists, do not reject these emotions out of hand. Confucians believe that one of the proper forms of cultivation is to discipline the emotions when they need to be restrained and to follow them when they need to be listened to. In fact, the most Confucian thing to do is to use the emotions for Confucian purposes of self-cultivation. Emotions, therefore, are viable means toward real sage learning; and because women have strong links to the emotional life, they can use these links to the emotions as the springboard towards self-cultivation. The women poets turned the male taunt that they were too emotional to their own advantage. How could one be too emotional if one were a proper Confucian? The problem was not with the emotions themselves, only in their proper cultivation. In this regard these "teachers of the inner chambers" had something profound to teach their fathers, brothers, husbands, and sons. Most of these educated women, however, distanced themselves from the wild teachings of the Taizhou school; Mrs. Li and her friends believed themselves to be models of Confucian self-discipline.

Yet in the end the whole experiment in expanding the range of Confucian teachings begun by Wang and his more radical Taizhou disciples was condemned as a mistake even by those who followed Wang's basic patterns of thought. When Chinese scholars tried to understand why the Ming dynasty had fallen prey to massive corruption and ultimately had been replaced by the Manchu Qing dynasty, they argued that seeds of social and intellectual decay could be traced directly to the teachings of Wang and his more radical students. The radicals in Wang's camp had gone too far in accepting the sweep of human emotion and by coming too close to the unworldly excesses of Chan Buddhism. If there were no social norms beyond the flux of human emotion, where could society find its foundations? Put simply, the Ming had too much self-expression for its own good and was ill-equipped to defend the country against the ravages of civil war.

Yet in the end, some Confucians showed that they could still link theory and action. The last great scholar of the Ming, the renowned Liu Zongzhou (d. 1645), proved this with the sacrifice of his own life. Although Liu had been a harsh critic of the failings of the Ming house, when it had fallen to the double blows of civil insurrection and the begin-· nings of the Manchu conquest, Liu rallied to the falling dynasty. A great philosopher who was a critic of both Zhu and Wang, he attempted to support the Ming. But when it was clear that the Ming cause was failing, he refused to move yet again in support of the Manchu emperor. He told his disciples that if he had followed the Ming claimants to the throne, people would think that he was now doing so for personal reasons. Rather, the great philosopher refused to eat and died among his students, a martyr to the Confucian vision of loyalty to the state even when the ruling house had lost the mandate of heaven.

Although Liu would not have approved of her, the famous and talented courtesan Liu Rushi (1618–64) tried to arouse some sense of patriotism in her male clientele for the support of the Ming cause. She could not understand why these young men were not more loyal to the dynasty that had provided them with official careers. She marveled at the fact that she understood loyalty while the men around her shirked their Confucian obligations. Confucius, himself still much closer to being a knight of the Zhou, probably would have been pleased to see Liu Rushi demonstrate that truly moral integrity was to be found in every human heart. However, most people were less sure about what to make of these audacious women scholars of the late Ming. The more restrained ladies of the Qing, although they continued to write poetry and provide Confucian education for their daughters and sons, were critical of the strange reversal in gender roles that haunted the late Ming.

In the Qing dynasty the intellectual tide had swung in the opposite direction. In the first place, there was a scholarly and official reaffirmation of Master Zhu's orthodox teachings. Secondly, there arose a whole new attitude towards the study of the Confucian Way known as "evidential research." As scholars pondered how the Way should be studied, it struck these Evidential Research scholars that both Master Zhu and Wang Yangming were wrong about both matters of historical and philological fact and the moral lessons to be drawn from Confucian scholarship. Zhu and Wang were both too much committed to metaphysical speculation. Although there was a difference between Zhu and Wang, both were captives of a philosophic, speculative turn that betrayed the Confucian Way. Many Qing scholars learned to doubt whether or not the whole grand philosophic project of the Song and Ming was really Confucian at all. If by Confucian we mean the actual thought of the early sages, then the Evidential Research scholars were dubious about the claims and counter claims of Zhu's *lixue* (School of Principle) and Wang's *xinxue* (School of Mind-heart).

The Qing scholars asked themselves, Why and what do we study? Do we do so in order to create complicated philosophic systems that resemble the fantasies of the Buddhists or Daoists? The answer should be no. A true Confucian is a person who studies reality as it really is in order to serve other human beings. We must find reality in the facts. This appeal to history, to finding reality in the facts of history and the early texts became the battle cry of the great Qing scholars. This search for the facts of history was organized in a number of ways, but metaphysical flights of fancy were not one of them. Confucius would never have approved of these Daoistic and Buddhistic forms of self-cultivation. Scholars needed to return to solid historical, philosophical, and scientific studies. It is better to study the history of economic policy or the hydraulics necessary for irrigation or the dredging of the Grand Canal. This is what the evidential scholars sought to do.

The first thing that the Evidential Research scholars did was to seek to return to the true sources of Confucian learning, the classics. The Evidential Research scholars were also known as the School of Han Studies. This name meant that they wanted to read the classics without the distortion provided by the Tang, Ming, and Song commentaries. It did not mean that they were moved by the great synthesis of Confucians such as Dung Zhongshu; quite to the contrary, the Evidential Research scholars argued that they needed to return to the scene of the crime, the earliest extant versions of the Confucian classics. Such a demand for a return to the best texts meant that they had to return to the Han texts – though they recognized that these Han texts were, in themselves, created long after the sages and masters had recorded them in the Shang and Zhou dynasties. Only by returning to the original Confucian sources, without any contamination from Buddhist and Daoist literature, could real scholarly progress be made. No one had ever paid more careful attention to the history and philology of the texts.

The second thing Qing scholars did was a return to the serious study of history and other practical sciences. The combination of philology and history gave them a better understanding of the true meaning of the early sages. It was a heady form of scholarship befitting the grand stature of the Qing state. Evidential Research scholarship was profoundly wedded to the past and yet poised to move forward. It sought truth in the facts; these facts would allow for true Confucianism to flourish again. Yet there were subversive currents. For instance, once one had begun to doubt the records of the Song and Ming philosophers, where did the doubt stop? Many of the Evidential Research scholars even doubted the classical texts themselves in an ironic way. In wanting to return to the pristine ancient texts they came to realize that they could never move beyond the work of the Han editors. How could one be sure that even the early Han texts accurately transmitted the Confucian Way?

It was a golden era for the study of local and regional institutions. The theory was that Confucians needed to return to their roots, to escape the mistakes of the Song and Ming thinkers. Idle metaphysical speculation should be replaced by attention to the sources of local and regional institutions. For instance, was it more important to reform the tax system or ruminate on the ethical cultivation of civil servants? While Confucians were always intensely interested in ethics, the Evidential Research scholars pointed out that you could only provide good government if you understood complex historical institutions such as tax policies. The same would hold for irrigation, plant science, and even forensic medicine.

Dr. Li reflected on the perennial Confucian insight that the Way was long and the burden of culture was heavy. Each generation had to reappraise the Way for itself. The task of Confucian history was not merely scholastic. It was actually to cultivate the Way. When viewed through the long lens of history, the Confucian tradition was a pageant of educated men and women seeking to realize the Way in their own lives in service to others. The forms and styles of such a quest varied widely over time and space and reflected the changing landscape of Chinese rich culture and its contact with foreign influences.

Plate 5 Animal sculptures in the Forest of Confucius probably represent pre- and peri-Confucian beliefs related to the fertility of herds and flocks, which in turn contributes to the well-being of humans and economic health. The animals' spirits also accompany the dead in the next world, just as they did in life. Photo: Evelyn Berthrong.

5 EXAMINING EVIL AND GOVERNING THE QUOTIDIAN

During the mid-morning Dr. Li had to face the most unpleasant part of his day, the forensic examination of two possible crime sites. After attending to matters of justice, he also must attend to some of the more quotidian aspects of his job as a city magistrate. The duties as a magistrate included the investigation of dubious deaths – either strange accidents or obvious crimes. It was the magistrate's responsibility to find the cause of death and to apprehend the criminal or criminals involved if it was a murder case. A Confucian magistrate was often called the father–mother of the people; he was also a policeman and judge. Dr. Li never liked the criminal investigations; there was nothing in the standard Confucian education that prepared a young magistrate for facing the corpse of a murder victim. Nonetheless, it was an official and weighty duty and this meant that any magistrate had to do the best he could.

Moreover, because of the nature of Qing law in capital cases, there was an automatic set of appeals that would wend their way to the emperor himself. In the Qing penal system, only the emperor could order an execution for murder. This meant that any magistrate investigating a capital crime such as murder had to be meticulous in the procedures followed in the investigation and in the preparation of the various legal documents detailing the results of the investigation. And even when the case was upheld at the highest levels, there was often a granting of amnesty to criminals.

However, Dr. Li's very practical father-in-law had provided him with a fascinating work on forensic medicine, among other manuals on local administration, that proved invaluable when he had to carry out various investigations of suspicious, unwitnessed deaths. One of the reasons that a local magistrate was expected to cover such a range of duties was pedagogical as well as practical. Confucian scholars as magistrates and as members of the imperial civil service were educated as generalists. Some Confucians believed that this was a partial mistake. At its best, the educational system turned out men who shared a common background and had a strong desire to serve the public and their emperor as best as they could. But this was just a hope. Practical skills had to be learned on the job; often this meant that a young official had to rely a great deal on the unofficial local staff, who, unlike him, had not passed through the official examination system, but who did have highly specialized knowledge of the workings of a local administration.

By posting young graduates of the examination system in jobs that exposed them to the full range of the duties of the civil service, it was further hoped that this would produce a corps of men with similar experience of all the various complex tasks of the imperial civil service. Even if a particular official would spend much more time later in his career in one particular area of government, such as taxation or education, each tyro official would have had exposure to the full range of bureaucratic concerns. The ideal of a gentleman-official, therefore, also had some practical benefits when and if the system actually worked. Just as the examinations made sure that the officials had the same basic education, postings in the provinces provided the new magistrates with a common set of experiences that allowed them to understand what went on at the lowest level of the imperial civil service.

Medicine, especially the knowledge of medicinal plants and herbs plus the diagnostic arts of traditional Chinese medicine, was considered a reasonable undertaking for a Confucian gentleman. Many of the best doctors in Suzhou were Confucian scholars. Not very many crafts or professions beyond governmental service were acceptable for study by a true Confucian gentleman. As Mencius had said so long ago, those who worked with their hands were ruled by those who worked with their minds. For the most part, Confucians did not engage in manual labor, although there were a number of scholars who believed that this lack of physical exercise was dangerous for the health of the scholar.

Although it was not an official classic, the earliest medical text was purportedly written by the Yellow Emperor for the benefit of the people. This meant that medicine was more than a technical art – it was a skill appropriate to a Confucian gentleman. As noted above, a few broadminded scholars disputed rejection of any physical work and reminded the Confucian community that Confucius was skilled in archery and charioteering. Still, the administration of a great empire demanded all kinds of technical skills that were not found in the philosophic texts that dominated the examination system.

Any new magistrate soon discovered that his literary education did not equip him for the rough and tumble of the administration of up to 250,000 souls. He was responsible for the smallest bureaucratic unit in the empire; hence he was also the end of the line of battle between government and the people. He was expected to set an example for his semi-professional staff and to work with the local literati. Both his office staff and the literati were local people. The goodwill of the local literati was crucial. By the Qing dynasty they carried out many quasi-governmental roles for the magistrate. If the magistrate had their respect, the literati could provide invaluable services and advice to the magistrate. Also by the time of the Qing, more scholars passed all the levels of examinations than there were jobs in the civil service. Qualified candidates often had to wait years for appointment. In some cases, talented degree holders might never actually receive an official appointment. Nonetheless, all of the local literati were part of the society of the learned. They were the social equals of the magistrate.

THE EVIL

Dr. Li wondered about the kind of scholar who could have written a book such as Song Zu's *The Washing Away of Wrongs*. It was an extremely useful account of how to examine bodies in order to discover if there had been foul play involved in the person's death. Although there were constables with a great deal of experience in such matters, the ultimate responsibility for the final report on the death resided in the hands of the magistrate if he were at all diligent about his official duties. Moreover, because these cases dealt with life and death judgments, all reports from the magistrate were carefully reviewed by the higher levels of the ministry of justice.

The Washing Away of Wrongs was a short book written in the Song dynasty (960–1279). It assumed that its reader was an educated man with some passing knowledge of the basic principles of medicine. It built upon the common medical lore of the Chinese people. Then the book expanded this lore into the realm of forensic medicine. It did not intend to make the magistrate into a skilled medical examiner; rather it aimed to provide him with enough information to form his own opinion about the cause of death and how to proceed if foul play was involved.

Although the two present cases were somewhat out of the ordinary, at least one did not immediately seem anything more than a tragic accident. The second case, however, was much more suspicious. Actually, as was proper in such matters, in the first case the local headman for the district claimed that the death was an accident. This was also a point where the local knowledge of the clerks was vital. First, someone like Dr. Li had to rely on their knowledge of the local people, including the headmen and ward elders. Dr. Li had to develop some trust in the veracity of his clerks. Second, Dr. Li would then have to sift the accounts of the local headman; of course, it was the local people who were first on the spot and who also would know any necessary and pertinent information about the deceased.

As Dr. Li walked to the site of the investigation of the purported accident, he thought about some of the other technical manuals he had begun to collect. Although this was not the kind of literature upon which classical Confucian culture was built, Dr. Li had become more and more interested in it over the years. Some of his interest was purely pragmatic, such as with the book on forensic medicine, but other genres simply appealed to his curiosity. Besides, had not Master Zhu argued that the examination of things was the beginning of self-cultivation? And there were so many fascinating things in the bustling world of seventeenth century Suzhou, though murder was not fascinating at all, especially when you had to examine the details of the crime and crime scene. Moreover, if it turned out to be a murder case, then it would be reviewed at the highest levels; if the magistrate made a mistake it would be a grave mark against his career. Only the imperial court had the power to execute even local criminals, a fact that Dr. Li kept carefully in mind.

A scholar-official such as Dr. Li was supposed to be a humanistic generalist. The classic tag was that a scholar was a gentleman of broad cultural vision and experience, a minister to a worthy prince, and not a utensil, i.e. someone only fit for technical service. He received his education in the Confucian classics, their commentaries, other classical literature, poetry, and history for the most part. Figuring out how to solve a murder case, trying to determine if a death was accidental on the basis of forensic evidence, or uncovering a clever Song bronze forgery of a Zhou wine vessel were definitely not part of the curriculum. Yet every official had to learn to deal with various physical aspects of the mundane world.

This need for more refined technical information was directly related to the typical career path of most scholar-officials. The model was for service in a broad range of appointments early in their careers. However, most officials, along with a general grasp of the essentials of Qing governance, actually tended to gravitate toward one bureau or another. Some became experts in finance; some in military procurement, some in irrigation and flood control. Some became expert in legal affairs.

The general philosophic approach to all of these practical administrative matters was subject to Confucian humanistic traditions in education. On the whole a scholar-official was not trained in technical matters, at least theoretically. However, any astute official recognized the need to understand the workings of the craftsmen who produced the myriad machines that made the country work. For instance, mining was essential to provide the metals for currency and weapons. Therefore, if you were assigned to a mining district, it was essential that you knew something about mining technology. For instance, you needed to understand the basic principles of the great pumps that kept the deeper mines from being flooded. Curiosity and the commandment to examine things were very much part of the Confucian tradition, and from time to time very respectable literati became fascinated with technical lore and would produce carefully crafted accounts of these artisan wonder-workings.

At this point, Magistrate Li arrived at the site of the accident. One workman had fallen from a city watchtower. The tower was used to look over the city and sound the alarm in case of fire. The workman had slipped off the roof, which he had been repairing just before the mishap. There were two general things to discover now. The first task was to check the roof to see if it really was an accident. It appeared that the workman had been alone when he fell to his death. Accompanied by the foreman of the repair company the magistrate went up to look at the roof. The foreman pointed out that the tiles on the edge of the roof were not as solid as they appeared to be. The water over the years had washed away the cement that held them in place. The workman, who obviously had not taken the time to examine the tiles carefully, had placed his foot on one such tile and it had given way. The only real blame is that no one was with him and that he had not tied himself to something more solid as he would have done normally.

The magistrate went on to ask a few more questions. Did anyone have an obvious reason to harm the workman? The unanimous response was that the workman was an honest and well-liked chap. No one could think of any possible reason that anyone would want to harm him. Nobody had warned the repair crew that the tiles were loose because no one knew when he had started his climb; in fact, nobody knew that the tiles were that loose till after the fatal fall. Of course, before the poor man had gone on the roof, no one had probably been to that part of the tower in years. Therefore, the magistrate would make the finding that the death was an unfortunate accident.

The second case was initially reported as a suicide by hanging. The body had been taken down and was lying on the floor of the small shed where the suicide was supposed to have taken place the night before. However, once the magistrate examined the body, it was clear to him that this was not a suicide at all but rather a murder. His police sergeant, who had gone to the site before Dr. Li, had suggested the same in his verbal report. Having already worked closely with this policeman before, Dr. Li tended to believe his surmise and was more than prepared to mount a more thorough investigation of the death.

The magistrate had read the second section of *The Washing Away of Wrongs* about what to look for on the neck of the victim when he heard that he had a hanging to investigate. The text gave very specific instructions about how to tell the difference between a suicide by hanging and more homicidal manners of death. He had decided to inspect the neck of the victim first before examining the place where the victim was found hanging. This would tell the magistrate whether this was a suicide or a possible crime.

By looking carefully at the bluish marks on the neck of the victim it was clear that he had not hanged himself, but rather had been strangled. The marks were much too low on the neck and too regular to have been caused by hanging. The victim very probably had been strangled or garroted from behind. After he had been killed, the body had been moved and hung from the beam of the small room. The magistrate did not even need to examine the rope or its fittings. This was obviously not a suicide.

At this point the investigation would take a different direction. It was essential for the sergeant to interrogate the family and cohorts of the victim in order to uncover the roots of the crime. This was a painstaking operation and would take more time than the magistrate had now. He would turn the preliminary work of the inquest over to one of his most trusted subordinates, namely the police sergeant. However, since this was now a murder case, he would have to remain personally vigilant about its outcome.

Actually, Dr. Li was presently writing the lengthy memorials that he would forward through the appropriate channels of the Bureau of Justice in another murder case. This was especially important, and not only because of the nature of the crime. In the particular case Dr. Li was writing about, it was hard to say that it was an outright case of murder, if murder is a crime of premeditated evil thoughts and heinous actions. Drunken brawls at a local tavern that ended in what was apparently an accident were difficult cases. They were murder in a technical sense, but needed to be reported carefully.

The second reason that Dr. Li was writing such an extended memorial was that any case demanding a possible execution would be reviewed at the national level; only the emperor could approve the execution of the criminal. Because the memorial would be reviewed by many levels of officials, including those who were very experienced in such matters, Dr. Li needed to use all of his skills in order to present the case. Although Qing officials were expected to be competent administrators across the whole range of government concern, many officials later in their careers were assigned to one specific bureau. Qing China did not have lawyers in the Western sense of a learned profession; however, many officials in the Bureau of Justice were skilled in the interpretation and practice of Chinese penal law. They would look very carefully at any memorial with implications for capital punishments.

Of course, it was not always the case that the emperor would personally review such cases. However, when such a man as Kangxi (r. 1662–1723) was on the throne, this actually did happen. The Kangxi emperor took his legal obligations seriously. He was an intelligent and often humane man; he was educated in the classical Confucian texts and his native Manchu customs. While the emperor could be harsh when the case dictated such a response, he could also be lenient. The emperor could grant pardons when he believed they were warranted. Ultimately, the power of life and death rested in his competent and shrewd hands.

One of the things that concerned the Confucian magistrates in criminal cases was that most crime was committed by young men. When studied carefully, young men between the ages of eighteen and about twenty-six were the worst offenders. The Chinese legal system recognized this and had devised ways to cope with the young male's proclivity to commit crime. The first hope was that, given strong guidance, reform was possible. There needed to be punishment for the act, but it was even better if the young man could be shown the error of his ways.

Chinese penal law was predicated on the expectation that the accused, once he (or she) had been shown to be completely guilty, would repent and deliver a sincere confession. In fact, no case was considered closed until a suspect confessed to the crime. Once this was done, then there was a chance for reforming the culprit. This hope for reform was based on at least two major Confucian principles. The first principle was the philosophic claim that human nature was basically good. Of course, this did not mean that everyone acted in the proper ethical fashion. Confucius had said that we all begin in the same place but diverge in practice. This rather cryptic comment was interpreted to mean that although our fundamental human nature was good, it could wander easily from the path of justice for a host of reasons. Human nature needed to be cultivated; and if a person committed a crime, part of this cultivation could be harsh punishment. Nonetheless, there was always the hope that, with the proper circumstances and education, that reform was possible.

The second principle was that no one could become the ethically virtuous person they ought to be without serious self-cultivation. One would hope that this cultivation would take place in the home and schools, but if not, then the state could also play a role through penal reform. One of the most needed things was to teach better work habits and life skills to these young men, though Dr. Li would have used the Confucian language of education and reform to describe what should go on in a properly run prison. Confucian education was, at least in part, based on a deep appreciation of the role of habit. For instance, one of the roles of a parent or teacher was to cause the child or student to act in a proper way, even if the child or student did not wish to act properly. Repeated proper actions, it was believed, could help to shape character. Conformity to ethical principle was a physical appetite as well as an intellectual achievement, or so the Confucian scholars believed. Doing good would make you not only a better person, but also a happier one. So correcting actions was as important as instilling solid principles.

Many young criminals, it was discovered, had little self-discipline. One of the aims of prison was to instill a new set of behaviors. Hard work was one method of achieving this end. Moreover, there had always been the belief that the prisoners should engage in some kind of constructive work. They would learn better work habits and help to pay for their own reintroduction into society. The tradition of prison labor had a hallowed place in the Chinese penal system. Reform and economic self-support were two pillars of the system.

Once a criminal had served a certain portion of his sentence, and if he demonstrated a willingness to mend his ways, he was often given a choice about how to finish his term of incarceration. For example, he would be offered the chance to volunteer for military service. If he went into the army, he would still be under discipline, but with a greater sense of freedom. He would also continue to learn how to work with other people. Once his tour of duty was completed, he would be set free to return to civil society.

The young man was now probably older than twenty-six and it was hoped that his experience in prison and the army would keep him out of further trouble. Of course, Confucian civil servants recognized that such reform would not work for all people. For hardened and violent criminals the state maintained what we could call maximum security prisons. The Chinese system of justice abhorred violent crimes. A person who committed a number of violent robberies could count on spending a very long time in penal servitude. Also, there was recognition of criminal insanity as well. Some people could probably never be trusted to return to society, both for their own good and for the good of other people. Last but not least, there were those who committed truly atrocious crimes, such as premeditated murder with malice aforethought. In those cases, capital punishment was merited and was meted out upon approval of the emperor.

Another feature of the Chinese legal system was the use of legal torture. If a judge believed a person was clearly guilty, torture could be applied to secure a confession. However, it was often clear to the legal officials that evidence collected under torture was not the best evidence. They noted that almost anyone would confess to a crime if they were tortured long and hard enough even if they were actually innocent of the charge against them.

THE MUNDANE

Dr. Li decided that he would attend to the more mundane tasks first. Because Suzhou was such a great city, items of all manner of goods in wonderful plenitude entered its gates. There were grains and teas, silks and cottons, spices and herbs, iron and silver, gold and jade, medicines and ink, fine papers and raw hemp. The government of China took an interest in taxing all of these items. Dr. Li's day was set aside for going over some pawnshop taxes. Prior to 1674, that tax rate had been set at five taels a year. However, due to the necessity of raising funds to suppress the Rebellion of the Three Feudatories, the tax had been raised to ten taels a year. Taxpayers were never happy with any levy; but they liked an increase in taxes even less.

However, there were benefits to paying taxes for the pawnshops. The proper payment allowed the owners to display a sign outside their doors. Of course, there was always the problem of trying to identify pawnbrokers who had or had not paid their yearly tax. The difficulty was that the pawnshop owner could choose to pay the tax directly to the provincial treasury. If he did so, then the owner would receive a receipt certifying the payment of the tax for the year. Checking on the payment was tricky because of the constant threat of unscrupulous local clerks. Many clerks took bribes from the shop owners so that they would be unreported.

One of the great problems of running a local government was the constant scrutiny needed to keep the local clerks in line. Though there had been myriad suggestions for reform over the centuries, the problem of the contests between the clerks and the magistrate was very serious. The root of the problem lay in the decision of dynasty after dynasty not to include the local clerks in the formal structure of government. Although the clerks were educated men, they were not holders of official degrees. This meant the local magistrate was in charge of a population of 250,000 plus people. Clearly the magistrate could not carry out all of his business without a host of local assistants.

The problem was even more complicated because of other aspects of the imperial civil service. The most vexing was the famous law of avoidance. The law of avoidance stipulated that no official could serve in his home province. The idea behind the law was simple; it was to make sure that an official would not be pressured by local family and friends into breaking the law. On the whole, most officials believed that it was a good policy. One of the downsides of the policy was that a magistrate could often be posted to a province where he did not speak the local dialect. Of course, the magistrate could always speak what the people called the Language of the Officials, which was basically the language of the majority of the people of North China. However, this did mean that the magistrate was effectively cut off from direct conversation with the local people. Moreover, officials were moved around fairly frequently, so just when a magistrate began to learn the local dialect, he was often transferred.

In order to get around the gap between the magistrate, representing the imperial government at the lowest level, and the population, it was necessary to employ a host of local clerks. The magistrates came and went, but the clerks remained in the Yamen (the official compound of the magistrate) for years and even decades. From time to time radical thinkers argued that the only way to deal with the problem was to include the clerks in the formal arrangements of government. Moreover, the generally low salaries of all government officials compounded the problem with the local clerks. With their salaries so low and with no prospect of ever being promoted into the regular civil service, the opportunities for bribery and corruption only multiplied.

Another aspect of the problem was that the salaries of the magistrates and officials were also low when compared to their expenses. This imbalance between the private and familial expectations of the official life and the reality of the actual salaries made it hard for even a basically honest man to escape some forms of corruption. The line between corruption and honesty was hard to chart. For instance, there were many irregular fees that were considered more or less licit and customary. Furthermore, what was the difference between a gift and a bribe? It was beyond the scope of any one official to deal with these problems.

The best that an honest official could do was to keep a careful eye on the local clerks. The problem, as mentioned before, was that the clerks were local people who understood the murky world of the interaction between Confucian ideals and administrative practice. Prudence dictated that no magistrate look too hard or too long at the practices of his clerks unless the clerks became too rapacious. Moreover, it was only the local clerks who really understood where local custom and the law came into conflict. If the magistrate wanted things to run smoothly, then he needed the support of the local clerks. Although the provincial and national governments were committed to honesty and rooting out graft, they were also eager to receive their tax quotas on time.

The relatively low salaries of the officials themselves were also a problem for an honest administrator. If the official came from a rich family, the pressure was less. But if the magistrate was the first son to rise so high from a poor family, the impulse to provide a better life for his extended family was immense. Officials were only too aware of the pitfalls of their life in government service. At any time they could make a mistake that could destroy their career. Or even if they did not make a bureaucratic mistake, they could end up on the wrong side of the political fence and consequently lose their jobs. So whether they liked it or not, the local magistrates had to rely on the services of the local clerks.

TECHNOLOGY AND FORGERY

One of the cultural areas that fascinated many Qing literati was the collection of antiques of all kinds. Some of these collections needed no real justification. Rare works of the calligraphy and painting of the past were part of the educated life of any elite scholar who could afford them. Libraries were also treasured repositories of any educated family.

Bronze vessels were among the most prized of antiques. First, they were a tangible connection between the early dynasties and the present empire. Some of them purportedly had been cast in the Shang and Zhou periods. Second, they were objects of great intrinsic beauty. Modern pottery, painting, and porcelain may have reached new heights under the Qing, but most collectors were of the opinion that the golden age of bronze work only lasted from the Shang to the Han (eighteenth to second century B.C.E.), and that the best bronze ritual vessels were the earlier ones. They were so precious that there was even a flourishing market for forgeries.

Dr. Li had seen some Song dynasty forgeries of Shang vessels and confessed that he was completely unable to tell the genuine from the fake. Of course, as with collecting all works of art, a keen eye, almost a sixth sense, was necessary. However, with the passage of time even fine Song forgeries became valuable artistic relics. Moreover, there was a body of literature that helped the novice collector of bronzes to make some basic choices between fakes and contemporary forgeries. Some of the advice was obvious. If a bronze had inscriptions in a style popular in the Song but unheard of in the Zhou, then the piece was clearly a fake.

The technical treatises went on to explain other bits of information. With patience one could learn to distinguish between the older and more difficult methods of classical bronze casting and simpler modern methods. Similar techniques were applicable to other forms of art objects as well. What fascinated Dr. Li all on its own was the technological literature itself.

All of these antiquarian and technical, and sometimes even legal, issues came together now for Dr. Li. A local dealer in ancient bronzes had just received a shipment of exciting new vessels. The major question among the literati collectors was, were these bronze vessels what they were purported to be? In this case, the dealer, who was a failed scholar from a good local family, was concerned to seek the guidance of a friend he shared with Dr. Li. The dealer had worked hard to gain a reputation for fair dealing. Because he came from a literati family, he had access to the elite of the city even if he personally had never entered the ranks of the civil service. Some would criticize him for engaging in a commercial venture, but at least everyone who dealt with him vouched for his honesty.

Dr. Li's friend was a recluse scholar. He had never passed the national examinations after having been very successful at the district and provincial level. This was common enough; many famous scholars had never passed the third leg of the examinations but had gone on to establish themselves as learned colleagues. In this case, because he came from a very wealthy and cultivated family, the friend in question had become a devoted collector of ancient bronzes. Over time he had also acquired the reputation of being a recluse. Dr. Li actually just thought he was naturally shy and not really averse to mixing with other serious literati collectors.

The collector had assembled, along with an outstanding array of bronze vessels, a wonderful library on the history of bronzes. For the most part, these were works for connoisseurs and not technical treatises on the art of ancient bronze making. However, as the collector explained, anyone who was seriously concerned about the provenance of bronze would soon have to learn a great deal about the actual casting of bronze objects. To this end, the collector had made several trips to visit contemporary metal working shops in order to see how the metal objects were made and to talk to the craftsmen about their skills. The collector discovered that many of the artisans were amused at the gullibility of many aesthetes. Although most of the artisans were illiterate, they could tell the collectors things about bronzes that were beyond merely artistic appreciation.

The dealer brought a number of objects to the meeting. As they went over the items one by one, they moved from the easy to identify to those that would take more time. For instance, he looked carefully at one piece, a rather nice one, and asked Dr. Li what he thought about its date. Dr. Li looked closely at the inscription on the bottom of the vessel and recognized it as a quote from the *Book of History*. Further, the graphs were cast in a very archaic script. Dr. Li finally said that this could probably be no earlier than the Han dynasty. In fact, this was what had been claimed for the piece when the dealer purchased it.

However, both the collector and dealer then smiled and explained why they both believed this definitely not to be a Han vessel. They brought in another piece and asked Dr. Li to observe the tiny casting marks around the legs of the piece. Both the dealer and collector said that they believed this to be a very early piece, perhaps early Zhou or even Shang. Dr. Li asked why they wanted him to notice the small marks in the bronze. They then asked him to look again at the vessel under consideration. Did he see any such marks? The answer was no.

The collector and dealer then decided that they had toyed long enough with their young friend. The collector explained to Dr. Li that there were many different ways to cast bronze. Bronze could be cast in pottery moulds or by what they called the lost wax method. They went into lengthy descriptions of the virtues of both processes. But then, they pointed out that all early bronzes were cast using the piece mould method. The early artisans certainly knew of the lost wax method but did not use it to cast their masterpieces. Rather, they had perfected the alternative, and much more complicated, piece mould method of casting the ritual bronzes.

Turning their attention back to the vessel under review, the collector and dealer then went on to show Dr. Li why anyone knowledgeable about bronze working would immediately realize that this piece was produced via the lost wax method. The conclusion was that this was not even a Han bronze because the lost wax method did not come into use until much later in the history of Chinese metallurgy. Dr. Li had been fooled by the crafty use of a classical text cast in a truly ancient form of the Chinese language.

But both the collector and dealer went on to point out that this forgery was from the Song period itself. In the Song dynasty the passion for collecting ancient bronzes had become intense. And where there is money to be made, there will be people who will try to take advantage of the unwary, especially in the world of art. Although this was a forgery, it was believed that it represented the work of a very accomplished forger, and hence had a value in its own right. Of course, as a forgery it was not worth anything like an actual Han dynasty original; nonetheless, it was worth more than Dr. Li would have guessed. But the price was low enough, so Dr. Li decided to buy the piece.

THE MATERIAL WORLD

In many respects, Dr. Li and his friends and family, as a Confucian elite, were lucky to live when they did. The long history of China and East Asia has known many renewals and golden ages. The last part of the seventeenth century in China was one of these times. It was a time of peace and cultural flourishing. As far as we can tell, it was about as prosperous as one could find anywhere in the world prior to the modern period. As the Chinese Confucians looked out over their world, they could take pride in what they saw. Commerce flourished; books circulated; brilliant scholars were developing radical new ways to understand their own history. As someone once pointed out, you were even likely to get much better medical care in China at this time than in Europe.

The problems that would plague China and East Asia in the nineteenth century during their confrontation with the colonizing west seemed but mere clouds on the horizon. The Qing empire was in a period of great expansion after Dr. Li's time. It was during the Qing period that Central Asia and Tibet were firmly welded onto the body of the empire. The Qing now controlled more territory than any other Chinese dynasty, save for the Mongol empire at its height, and the Mongols never really considered themselves a purely Chinese empire. Of course, the Manchu rulers of China also knew that they were not Chinese, but this did not matter as much to them as it might seem at the end of the seventeenth century. Ethnicity was not as important, though many Chinese probably would have preferred a Chinese ruling house. But during the middle of the nineteenth century, when great rebellions racked central and southern China, it was the Confucian elite that rallied to the defense of the Manchu dynasty. What was important was the defense of "this culture of ours."

Our review of the varied administrative duties of Magistrate Li could be expanded to include many other things as well. The question of taxation, for instance, was always a crucial one for the Chinese state. The perennial debate was over how much could the state claim from the economy and the people and still allow some measure of economic flourishing. And once the amount had been set, there was the equally perennial battle to collect the taxes.

Viewing the early Qing world through the eyes of the Confucian elite also has its built-in blinders. For instance, the world would have looked very different through the lens of a poor peasant family eking out a meager existence in the northwest of China. But even the lives of the vast number of peasants varied across China. In the more prosperous parts of the Yangtze valley or the southeast, a rich peasant could own more and more land and become a rich landowner. At this point, money would then be invested in the education of sons to take the examinations. It was clear that the best way to fame and fortune in Qing China was via the examination system.

Or we could have tried to see the world through the eyes of rich merchants. As we shall see in the case of Japan, merchants founded their own schools. Some merchants in China became immensely wealthy. Great salt dealers and bankers rubbed shoulders with the literati elite; yet here again these merchants would seek to educate their sons for the examinations and to buy land. The salt dealers were granted special trading privileges and were able to create great fortunes. Yet once they had done so through their control of an essential market, they too had to seek the constant protection of the literati and sent their sons off to study for the examinations. Here again land and examination success were deemed the only safe way to secure the future of a family. Yet many of these merchants and artisans knew things at the core of Chinese culture that were unknown to the literati elite. For instance, the elite loved the fine porcelain produced for home and foreign export, but few mandarins knew much about how the translucent objects were actually made. The elite mandarins only knew how to tax the profits of the business. In short, the late Confucian world was a socially complicated place.

It may seem odd to pick something as artistically and technologically arcane as the forgery of ancient bronzes. Much more mainstream technical arts such as astronomy or calendrical reform would have served just as well. Both astronomy and the fixing of an accurate calendar were of great concern to the Chinese empire. Astronomy was closely related to astrology, and the traditional Confucians believed in a cosmos where one ought to pay attention to the messengers in the stars. There was a well-developed theory of astronomical portents that the emperor needed to monitor. Good omens were fine and demonstrated that the emperor and his civil service were governing well; evil omens were seen as signs warning the emperor that all was not well with his kingdom. Likewise an accurate calendar was crucial in an agrarian society. Timely planting of crucial crops often depended on the official calendar and almanacs.

The Confucian Way encompassed all of these diverse facets of life. It included a love of ancient bronzes, a desire to see justice done, and a wonderment about the stars. Confucians also thought a great deal about how to promote human flourishing. They were as dedicated to education as a means to advance human society as any people, and probably more so than most. Whatever else the New Confucian world will be, it will be an empire of learning.

The Confucians often remarked that their task was to preserve "this culture of ours," or to follow the Confucian Way. When Christian missionaries encountered Confucians for the first time, they engaged their East Asian colleagues in endless debates about the nature of their "religion." While it was clear to the missionaries that Buddhists and Daoists had religions, which the missionaries did not like one whit, the case of the Confucians was unclear. Every time the missionaries thought that they could pin down the religious dimension of Confucianism, the Confucians would wander off into hydraulic engineering or the like. The Confucians quite seriously told the missionaries that their concern for good irrigation was just as much part of their extended worldview as anything else, including the imperial worship of heaven in Beijing's great temples. As Herbert Fingarette so brilliantly summarized the Confucian viewpoint, the secular is the sacred.

From the perspective of the modern world, now set on moving into a new century and millennium, the Confucians sound remarkably "modern" when compared to the early Christian missionaries. The values of the Confucians, when translated into the context of modernity, look much like the values of the modern ecumenical new world order. This is true as far as it goes. For instance, the new economic and intellectual world depends on information. Information now flows endlessly around the world via printed texts and vast amounts of electronic data. The Confucians loved information. They also loved to ponder what the information told them. Moreover, the Confucians realized that to understand complex information, such as the ancient classics (and now the mysterious complexities of fractals and the Internet), education was crucial. Confucians applied these concerns for information and education to everything from the mundane to the sacred, and this is what makes classical- and Neo-Confucianism seem so modern.

Nonetheless, Confucian habits of the heart are still lurking behind the most advanced computer programs. As the Neo-Confucians liked to say, the principle may be one, but its manifestations are many. In order to find the true principles of the many in the modern world, Confucians also recall two other axioms for a balanced education. The first is the way of study and reflection. The second is the ethical, almost mystical, task of reverencing the virtuous nature. Most Confucians agree that only when both reflection and reverence are combined can we call a person an educated person. Only such a cultivated person is worthy of preserving and expanding "this culture of ours."

Amidst the constant flow of information, Confucians will always ask, how does all this information affect humanity? Does it help education? Does it help the development of the moral life? One must always pay attention to the world and yet not let the mass of data and things upset the commitment to human virtue and human flourishing. These three elements will surely inform the continuing Confucian contribution to the new ecumenical world culture.

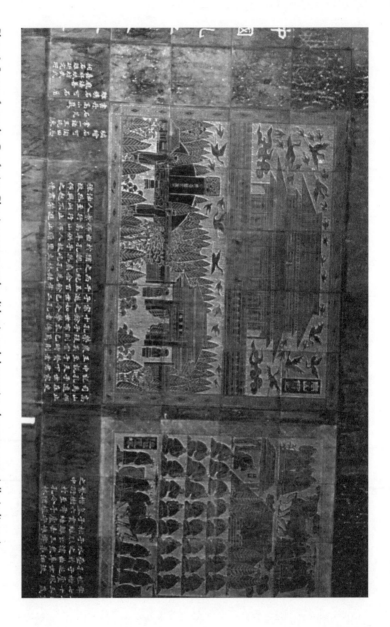

Plate 6 *Scenes from the Confucian Classics were popular didactic and decorative elements, especially in literati compounds and as here, in the walls of a foyer beside a gateway in the Forest of Confucius. These Classics were first translated by European missionary scholars in the seventeenth century.* Photo: Evelyn Berthrong.

6 MEETING A WESTERN SCHOLAR

That evening after he left the Yamen compound, Dr. Li made his way across the city to join his good friend Dr. Yao at a fine restaurant. This was more than an ordinary dinner party. Dr. Yao had invited the strange new barbarian scholar from the Far West to join with other scholar-officials. Along with purportedly being fine scholars of the classical texts, these exotic Western barbarians were priests of a new religion. They called their religion the Teaching of the Master of Heaven. They had new and interesting things to say about the geography of the world, the classical texts, and calendrical reform among other things. They were purported to be great mathematicians too.

Dr. Li was intrigued by the arrival of these learned men from the West. Actually, the Christian tradition had been in China at least since the Tang dynasty. In fact, the great Tang had thought so highly of the new religion that they had issued an edict of toleration. The same toleration to preach, teach, and practice was granted by the Qing dynasty as well. Nonetheless, it struck the Chinese literati as odd that such men would travel so far from home. Why would these barbarians risk so much to leave home and family? But then, didn't the Middle Kingdom always exert an attraction on the barbarians beyond its borders? Yet there were few barbarians who could be counted as scholars as these men seemed to be. The only exceptions had been some learned Buddhist monks from India. There was no doubt that the Buddhist merchants and missionaries had transformed the Chinese world. Perhaps the strange Western scholars were harbingers of a similar transformation, though no one gave this more than a passing thought. Never had the Chinese world been more secure or more expansive than it was in 1685.

Nonetheless, Dr. Li was aware that Buddhism had been a great Western import. Confucian scholars had mixed feelings about Buddhism, and Daoism for that matter. Many Confucian scholars loved to read the more refined Daoist and Buddhist literature. For instance, it was unthinkable not to be entranced by the beauties of Zhuangzi's great book of wonderful and strange stories or of Laozi's little classic. Confucians knew these texts as well as they did their own classics. Furthermore, the Daoists also shared other texts, such as the *Book of Changes*, with their Confucian cousins. The *Changes* belonged to all Chinese intellectuals. Each school battled to demonstrate how the great classic of divination was in line with their particular school of thought. Dr. Li had read numerous Daoist and Buddhist essays that tried to show that their philosophies were congruent with the *Changes*.

Many Confucian scholars believed that Buddhism and Daoism were fine for the common people and women, treating them as something less refined and worthy of attention. Of course, Confucian toleration did not extend to any kind of undue political action on the part of sectarian Daoists or Buddhists. Religious heterodoxy was possible but not confrontation with the state based on sectarian religious convictions. In fact, Confucian scholars had always viewed a great deal of the religious life of the Chinese common people as superstition. Xunzi went farther than most, and in his disregard for popular religion he did not contravene the other great classical masters. For Xunzi, the spirits were just manifestations of the vital force of the world. Although they might seem real to the ignorant, they were not living beings but forces of nature. They were not proper objects of study for refined gentlemen.

Honor the spirits but keep them at a distance – this was a good summary of Confucian views about other religions. At worst these religions were the grossest forms of superstition; at best they were harmless and simple ways for the common people to express their spiritual longings for a better life, immortality, or rebirth in another world. Most Confucian magistrates would not bother with regulating popular religion as long as it posed no problem for public order. This was especially the case when a religion, even a new one like Christianity, was formally recognized by the imperial government. However, if a religious group became politically involved, or demonstrated inordinate desires to turn their utopian dreams into physical reality, it was the duty of the magistrate to keep a careful eye on the group.

Ever since the Han dynasty imperial Chinese governments instituted bureaus of religious affairs in some manner or another. The purpose was not strictly to regulate novel or even strange religious ideas, though that could happen. The prime intent was to keep an eye on religious groups to make sure that they did not wander too far away from their specific religious concerns. The experience of the Chinese state ever since the rebellions of religious Daoist groups at the end of the Han (c. 180–200 C.E.) made the governments nervous about the chaotic potential of popular religious fervor. There was a delicate line between legitimate religious actions and associations and rebellion against the Confucian social order.

The arrival of Buddhism only complicated the issue of religion, society, and the state. In the first place, Chinese intellectuals had never confronted such a civilized tradition before. Actually, when Buddhism first arrived many Chinese thought that it was just another form of Daoism. In fact, there was an interesting story about this. The Daoist myth told of the departure of Laozi to the West. The theory was that Laozi taught Daoism to the Western barbarians and they turned it into Buddhism. The odd theory had some early appeal because religious Daoism was the only established and organized part of the Chinese religious scene that resembled Buddhism at all. However, it quickly became apparent that Buddhism was not just an Indian and Central Asian form of Daoism.

For many centuries Buddhism engaged the best minds of the Chinese world. The transformation was not confined to intellectual matters. The Buddhists brought with them a commitment to monastic life, a form of religious culture never seen before in China. Not only was monasticism something strange, it also challenged the very roots of Chinese culture: monks and nuns were celibate. This was unheard of in classical and medieval China. Chinese culture assumed that everyone would marry and form a family. Even those people who did not marry were still part of a family. From the Confucian point of view one of the gravest of all sins was not to have children to carry on the family line.

In fact, many scholars had noticed that Confucianism grew out of the Chinese family system. Critics argued that Confucians idealized family life, and that Confucian rhetoric about the emperor being the father and mother of the people was a myth that rarely coincided with reality. Even the major Confucian virtues, no matter how transformed through centuries of philosophic debate, were obviously generated out of the family. The virtue of *ren* or humaneness was supposed to be manifest in the love and respect between a father and son, mother and daughter. The family was the matrix of Confucian education and culture. Dr. Li knew that his wife took her role as the first teacher of Confucian virtues to his sons and daughters with utter seriousness. Mrs. Li was an educated Confucian lady who was a true Confucian teacher of the "inner quarters" of his family compound.

Of course, not all literati families were models for the nurture of Confucian virtue. Confucius himself recorded more than enough information about dysfunctional families although he had nothing to say about foreign religions per se. However, what was important was not whether a particular family followed the norms of proper civility. What people chose to believe in private was more or less their own business. Nonetheless, from the Confucian point of view it was crucial to bring order to the family and it was hard to see how this could be done on the basis of Daoism or Buddhism. Confucianism was the cornerstone for any civil society and has been so ever since the Han dynasty.

The Buddhist monastic institution challenged the Confucian family by suggesting that there was a radically different human social organization. This was the monastic road to liberation or what the Buddhists called nirvana. In fact, the Buddhists argued that one literally had to leave the family altogether in order to achieve liberation. The family was too emotional a place for the development of Buddhist insight for most people. Some Buddhist teachers taught that a lay person could achieve Buddhist liberation, but this was rare indeed. Most Buddhists, if they were really serious, needed to leave the family and become a monk or nun.

In the early development of the Buddhist monastic orders there was a great deal of debate about what the proper relationship between the monasteries and the rest of Chinese society should be. There was an interesting early case about whether or not a monk should bow to the emperor. In India this would be unheard of. A monk, even a junior monk, would never be forced to bow to a king. The theory was that the monk had passed beyond the confines of civil society. The debate raged in China for a long time. Some argued for bowing, but in the end new forms of social interaction were developed that honored both Buddhist piety and the norms of Confucian civil society. The Buddhists were eager to demonstrate that they were not antinomians or hostile to good government; they were simply those who had renounced any interest in what they called the "red dust" of the mundane world.

The other great question had to do with what became of filial piety in the Buddhist context. Filial piety was so much a part of Chinese culture that the Buddhists felt the need to come to terms with this primordial foundation of virtue and human life. One of the ways Buddhists did so was to point out that their prayers and lives of austerities actually were of great merit for the whole family of humankind. Their life of renunciation was a higher form of filial piety that would increase religious merit for all people, including the immediate family of the monk or nun.

One day Dr. Li even heard a Buddhist monk quote the famous second chapter of *The Classic of Filial Piety,*

> The Master said: He who loves his parents does not dare to hate others. He who reverences his parents does not act contemptuously toward others. By love and reverence being perfectly fulfilled in the service of his parents, his moral influence is shed upon the people and he becomes a pattern for all the border nations. This is the filiality of the Son of Heaven. The Code of Fu says: When the one man has goodness, millions of his people rely on him (Makra, 1961, p.5)

The Buddhist monk explained that in perfecting the good works inherent in the cultivation of the Buddha's law the monk or nun was actually loving and revering his or her parents more perfectly than the ordinary lay person. This was viewed as sophistry by the Confucians because filial piety also meant that one of the most unfilial things a person could do was not to have a family. This was a hard saying for the Buddhists because of their vows of celibacy.

The whole Buddhist approach was predicated on the reciprocal laws of karma and rebirth. The Buddhists taught that for every action there is a reaction. Good deeds generate good karma and bad deeds evil karma. In the complex theologies of Mahayana Buddhism, merit could be transferred from one person to another. A great monk or nun could literally help the less fortunate on their path to final liberation. While the effect of all this monastic virtue might not be efficacious during the present life, it could help others find a better form of rebirth. The Buddhists believed that we are born again and again until and unless we reach the other shore of nirvana. Only then does the cycle of rebirth and suffering end for the person. Needless to say, Confucians often disputed some or all of these Buddhist teachings. Confucians often recognized that the concern for rebirth did reinforce ethical behavior on the part of the Buddhist monks, nuns, and laity.

Many of the same Confucian objections were deployed against the Daoist religious sects as well. They were acceptable until and unless they moved into the political sphere where they did not belong. There was always the memory of the great Daoist revolts that helped to end the Han dynasty. Furthermore, Confucians believed that Daoism, at least at the popular level, pandered to the superstitious nature of the common people. It was not the job of the Confucian magistrates to stamp these religions out, but to provide more and better education so that people would not be drawn to these heterodox sects. It was often hard for an orthodox Confucian to distinguish between learned Daoists and popular religion.

What made dealing with religion even more difficult was that many people, especially since the middle of the Ming dynasty, were drawn to the theory of the unity of the three teachings. By this they meant that Confucianism, Daoism, and Buddhism were not considered mutually exclusive teachings but different aspects of the larger Way. A person, therefore, could choose to be a part of all three at once or mix them to suit their needs and abilities. One could be a Confucian in the office, a Daoist poet while drinking with friends, and a Buddhist when sitting in meditation.

In terms of the three teachings, Confucianism was recognized as the teaching most appropriate to family and civil life. No one would gainsay the role that Confucians played in education and the civil service. This was the teaching of the elite families. On the other hand, Daoism was more appropriate for those who, for whatever reasons, chose to with- draw from society. There is even a popular saying that goes, "a Confu- cian in office, a Daoist in retirement." Other scholars even preferred to follow the Daoist methods of self-cultivation that aimed at extending life. There was also the undeniable literary and artistic power of the great Daoist philosophic texts.

The Daoist religious communities and sects built on the early philo- sophic works and expanded their range; the religions developed elabo- rate mythologies, theories of salvation, and practices aimed at achieving long life and ultimately, bodily immortality. The religious Daoist schools were the indigenous Chinese counterparts to the great Buddhist temples and monasteries. They provided a refuge for people who cared to walk the paths outside regular society. They provided chants and spells for the common people. For the literati scholars the great Daoist sects promised union with the Dao. They were the fonts of the mystical tradition of the Chinese people. By the Qing period, the Daoists had produced a huge corpus of writings that almost equaled the Buddhist scriptures. This vast collection of texts had been revealed to Daoist luminaries for centuries, but most during the medieval period.

Nonetheless, it was the Buddhists who provided the greatest intellectual challenge to the Confucians. The Buddhists provided an alternative reading of reality. As the Confucians claimed, their teaching was based on reality as something concrete, while the Buddhists and Daoists taught about reality as emptiness and *wu* (nothingness). Although the teachings were different, this did not mean that the three teachings and their followers did not get along with each other. Often the great Buddhist abbots and Daoist masters came from the same social class as the Confucian literati. Daoist temples and Buddhist monasteries provided places for spiritual retreat for many a weary Confucian.

Moreover, there were many sincere Confucians who also considered themselves Buddhists. The great poet and scholar Su Shi (mid-twelfth century) of the Song dynasty was a perfect example of this mixing of traditions. Although recognized as one of the leaders of the Neo-Confucian revival, he loved Buddhist poetry and lore as much as his Confucian classics. Su saw no reason why he could not follow both paths. The notion that the boundaries between and among the religious teachings were completely sealed was alien to the Chinese sensibility. Although a person probably had a main tradition, he or she could call upon the other teachings in a time of need or to solve a particular ritual problem. The boundaries of Chinese religious life were porous.

Of course, there were people who held firmly to their respective religious traditions. Buddhist monks and Daoist priests were expected to follow the teachings of their own traditions. Many stalwart Confucians also would not mix their Way with other ways. Nonetheless, Dr. Li was persuaded by the work of many Evidential Research scholars that even the most orthodox of Confucians had borrowed from other traditions at various times. Perhaps it would be more accurate to say that such interaction happened at two distinct levels. The first evidenced clear borrowing of motifs, themes, and ideas from other traditions. For instance, it was obvious that Confucian poets would borrow such material from Buddhist and Daoist colleagues. They would not consider this borrowing in any way as a diminution of their commitment to the Confucian Way.

The second level had to do with general cultural influences. These were harder to ascertain and prove to be cases of direct borrowing. A perfect instance was Master Zhu's use of principle and vital energy to describe the formation of events and objects. Although the terms for principle and vital energy were very much part of the classical Confucian tradition, some scholars held that the proximate location for Zhu's usage came from the great Tang Buddhist thinkers in the grand traditions of Huayan and Tiantai. It was in the complicated metaphysics of these great Buddhist philosophic schools that scholars worried about the relationship of forms of order or principle and its ingression into vital force. At least the prototype of Master Zhu's theory about principle and vital force could be traced not to the history of Confucian thought but directly to the philosophic problems of the Buddhist dharma.

Dr. Li recognized the strength of the argument, but wondered what it really proved. At one level all it demonstrated was that the Buddhists had raised certain philosophic and cosmological questions that the Confucians needed to respond to. Of course there was nothing mysterious about such intellectual interaction. It happened all the time between and among thinkers of the same school as well. All we had to do was to remember the intense debates that Xunzi had with Mencius about the definition of human nature to see how such borrowing happened. Dr. Li was more inclined to credit a theory of stimulus or influence rather than any direct borrowing. However, the line between borrowing and stimulus was a fine one.

For instance, Master Zhu had admitted that, as a young man, he had read extensively in Daoist and Buddhist materials. But once he had accepted a Confucian teacher in Li Tong, Zhu gave up his Daoist and Buddhist studies. However, Zhu still loved to quote the Daoist philosophic classics from time to time and they surely remained part of his capacious memory. How could anyone not love Zhuangzi and Laozi for the poetry of their insights and the wonder of their strange tales? Likewise, no tradition in China had thought more about the cultivation of the mind-heart than the Buddhists. The Buddhist reflections on the illumination and awakening of the mind-heart became part and parcel of the language of all educated Chinese, Confucians included.

A perfect case in point, and one that would surely be part of the conversation with the Western scholars tonight, was Master Zhu's theory of the Supreme Ultimate. The crux of the contentious issue was not so much around the term Supreme Ultimate itself. The term occurred in the *Book of Changes*, an impeccable Confucian canonical classic. The problem came when Zhou Dunyi linked the Supreme Ultimate to the Ultimate of Nonbeing or nothingness in the first sentence of his *Diagram of the Supreme Ultimate*. Almost as much ink was spilled on this short sentence as had been expended on the first line to Laozi's philosophic poem. What did Zhou have in mind philosophically? And where did he get the term "Ultimate of Non-being?"

For once the philosophic problem was less difficult. What both Zhou and Zhu were trying to point out is that there is a profound and mysterious, truly vast, dimension to the Way that cannot be made simply into something finite, no matter how vast that one thing was taken to be. There is always more, namely the infinite nature of the cosmos. Of course, Dr. Li knew that this was a vast subject in and of itself. This kind of writing and philosophy, the mixture of terms taken from different sources in service of a philosophic system, was suspect from the viewpoint of the Evidential Research scholars (fl. seventeenth to nineteenth centuries).

The second question revolved around the provenance of the term Ultimate of Non-being (*wu-ji*). The Evidential Research scholars pointed out that this was, in all likelihood, a term borrowed from Daoist sources by Zhou. It was known that Zhou was familiar with such pre-Song Daoist sources. The Evidential Research critique was subtle; they pointed out that language, especially when used philosophically, had innocent meanings. Terms carried their histories with them. If you used a Daoist term, even with the best of Confucian intentions, you ran the risk of importing into Confucian thought a conceptual viewpoint that did not belong there. What, for instance, the Evidential Research scholars asked, did a Daoist idea about Ultimate Non-being have to do with solid Confucian teachings? From their point of view, it was a term and a corrupted teaching that should be excluded from the Confucian Way.

Dr. Li found it fascinating that some of the radical textual scholars of his day dared to doubt the historical accuracy of the traditional account of Confucius' authorship and editorship of the classics. Moreover, they pointed out that even Master Zhu in the Song dynasty had harbored scholarly reservations about the pristine accuracy of some of the canonical texts. Dr. Li realized that once the seed of a solid, careful scholarly doubt had been planted in his mind he had to admit that there was a real measure of truth in what the critics were saying about the traditional account of the compilation of the Confucian classics.

For instance, the philosophically famous "Sixteen Character Teaching" concerning the mind-heart, transmitted from the great Yu, as recorded in the *Book of Documents* was a perfect example of the problems of textual transmission. The text said "The mind-heart of man is insecure; the mind-heart of the Way is barely perceptible. Have utmost refinement and singleness of mind. Hold fast the Mean." Even Master Zhu had surmised that this famous short precept on the cultivation of the all too fragile mind-heart was of suspicious provenance. Nonetheless, Master Zhu continued to use the text because he thought it illustrated the difference between our natural or undisciplined mind-heart and the mind-heart of the Dao itself. The message was clear to Master Zhu: we need to cultivate carefully our human mind-heart of flesh and blood in order to conform it to the mind-heart of the Way. Only then can we move forward on the path of the Dao, even if this demands that we learn to doubt the history of the tradition itself from time to time. But from what perspective do we doubt? The whole question of authorship in the early days was difficult to prove. What was more important was the idea, the message of the mind-heart itself.

Oddly enough, the barbarian scholars agreed in part with the Evidential Research scholars on the issue of the misuse of Confucian texts by the Song dynasty revivalists. The conversation about these matters came up after the fine dinner. Dr. Li was impressed with the culture of the main guest, Dr. Ma Lipo (Fr. Malipiero). He was dressed as a scholar and spoke excellent Mandarin and demonstrated a wide familiarity with the Confucian classics and history. The first part of the evening had focused on questions to Dr. Ma about his country of origin. Dr. Ma said that he originally came from I-da-li (Italy) and had studied in the city of Luoma (Rome) both as a priest and as a scholar. His country and city were on the other side of the world and it had taken Dr. Ma almost a year to sail to Canton. He had been in China for over twenty years.

Dr. Ma followed a religious teaching that Dr. Li had not encountered before, the teaching of the True Lord of Heaven. Dr. Ma had given Dr. Yao a copy of a famous book on these teachings by the famous Dr. Li (Fr. Ricci) of a previous generation. Dr. Li had the opportunity to read the work quickly and he had to admit that it contained solid scholarship along with some rather strange interpretations as well. It was these strange interpretations about the nature of *tian* that fascinated both Fr. Malipiero and his Chinese friends.

Fr. Ma (as his Chinese friends would call him), following the interpretation of the teachings of the True Lord of Heaven, began by reviewing certain key texts in the early classics. He argued that the sages had indeed had knowledge of the True Lord. This was clear when you examined the passages about heaven in these texts. The sorrowful part was that this correct teaching about the role of heaven had been lost over the centuries. In fact, it had been completely replaced in the Song dynasty by the teachings of the School of Principle. Fr. Ma maintained that the name of this school was even wrong. What Master Zhu really taught was a form of materialism without any recourse to the true knowledge of heaven as a personal divine reality. Dr. Li countered that Master Zhu was aware of these early texts but interpreted them in a rational way rather than giving them over to some anthropomorphic reading. When asked about such matters once, Master Zhu said that there was no such thing as a great grandfather in the sky with a white beard.

The conversation was a fascinating one. The Western scholar was implying that he could provide a better reading of the early texts than Master Zhu. This was audacious, yet Dr. Li and his friends had to agree that Fr. Ma did make some good points. They would have to think again carefully about what the early texts said about heaven without immediately interpreting them in light of Master Zhu's understanding. Fr. Ma disagreed with the late Ming critics of Zhu as well. It appeared that this was a crucial point for Dr. Ma. Rather like some learned Daoists, he held that highest heaven was controlled and ordered by a supreme God or spirit. Dr. Li had always thought that there was something mysteriously profound about the ultimate nature of the Dao, but he was not prepared to accept that the Way was some kind of a person. That seemed a step too far.

The more difficult point had to do with the charge of materialism. Dr. Li could not see what the Western scholar was driving at until they began to talk about the role of vital force along with principle. There was no problem with the notion of principle because Fr. Ma said that his True Lord of Heaven was the divine lawgiver of the world. However, Fr. Ma had difficulty in understanding the nature of vital force. He seemed to assume that it must be purely material and concrete. The Chinese tried to explain what vital force meant, but there was little success in coming to any agreement. Fr. Ma was amazed to hear that even the incorporeal spirits were constituted by vital force. Fr. Ma maintained that something had to be material or spiritual and could not be both at one moment; the Chinese scholars patiently tried to explain that this was not the way vital force worked in Master Zhu's system. Dr. Li felt that both sides were missing something in the argument.

When it was clear that they would not make any more progress on the question of the role and nature of vital force, the discussion moved on to other topics. Because there had been many good drinks already, one of the Chinese friends dared to ask Fr. Ma about some of the strange social customs of the Western world. For instance, he had heard that even respectable ladies, the wives of scholars and princes indeed, were allowed to join in the company of men at dinner parties. How could such a thing happen? It violated all the known rituals of civilized life.

Fr. Ma calmly answered that different countries had different customs. For instance, in his native land of Italy, ladies never bound their feet. He conceded that Western women had more freedom outside of their houses than did Chinese ladies. Moreover, some Western countries were even ruled by queens. All of this seemed very strange to Dr. Li. He thought of his own wife and how appalled she would be if she had to attend such large dinner parties with all these strange men. On one point Dr. Li agreed with Fr. Ma. He believed strongly in the education of women and was providing the best tutoring he could find for his two daughters. Most of the early education was provided by his wife, herself an erudite Confucian woman who had received a fine education from her own mother and by female tutors provided by her father. Customs indeed differed from country to country, though the Confucian scholars were without doubt that their customs represented the highest form of human life.

The Confucian worldview was never self-consciously a missionary enterprise. Although Confucianism had become an international movement in East Asia, it had never done so as a missionary movement. Vietnam, Korea, and Japan had developed their own forms of Confucianism as part of the general package of imported Chinese culture. We must remember that China was the source of elite culture for the whole East Asian region. The only major non-Chinese exception was Buddhism. However, Buddhism itself had rapidly become very Chinese by the sixth and seventh centuries. The great empire of the Tang had been like a magnet to the emerging nations of East Asia. Tang China was one of the high points of world civilization, and Confucianism was definitely an essential part of the culture. As time went on, and as Vietnamese, Korean, and Japanese scholars continued to import Chinese books and ideas, Confucianism became an even more important aspect of East Asian culture. Confucianism, due to the revival of thought during the Song dynasty, replaced Buddhism as the foremost intellectual tradition in the whole region. As Vietnam, Korea, and Japan gradually developed their own culture, and as trade increased, the import of Confucianism continued apace. Just as Paris, London, and New York are considered great centers of culture, the smaller nations of East Asia gravitated towards the Chinese center and many extra-Chinese intellectuals became great Confucian scholars.

Still, the movement was motivated by the Vietnamese, Koreans, and Japanese seeking Confucian culture as the mark of mature civilization. This fitted very well with the sino-centric view of most Chinese intellectuals; namely that China was the absolute center of world culture. It was entirely proper for people from afar to come to China seeking trade and culture. However, it never struck the Chinese, save for a few Buddhist monks, that they could profit from leaving China. It was not the role of a Confucian scholar to travel to foreign lands. If the barbarians wanted to come to China and learn culture, that was acceptable. It made sense to the Chinese to have people travel to them for trade. The Chinese did not perceive that there was much in the outside world that was of much value to them. This was generally the case economically, and even more so culturally.

Although irenic Confucian scholars were impressed with the scholarly accomplishments of the Jesuit missionaries, not very many would accept the new faith. What excited the Confucians most of all was the scientific skills of the Jesuits, especially in astronomy and military manufacture. Open-minded Confucians had to agree that the Jesuit mathematical skills were superior to those the Chinese were using for their calendar. The Qing government was even willing to appoint Jesuits to positions responsible for the promulgation of the official calendar.

Some Confucians were even moved by classical scholarship of Jesuits like the great Matteo Ricci. However, most would have thought it ludicrous to convert to the new religion. If anything the Confucians assumed that the Jesuits would come around to the Confucian viewpoint given enough time in China. That someone like Fr. Ma was so skilled in Confucian texts seemed to prove the point. Although the Confucian literati were fascinated by the erudition of the Jesuit missionaries, few saw any reason to convert to the new Western religion. However, Dr. Li did know that some scholars, including some leading court officials, had been convinced enough by the arguments of the missionaries that they had become followers of the Lord on High.

CONTROVERSY OVER THE RITES

It was at this point that the conversation took another fascinating turn. One of the Chinese scholars reported another odd encounter that he had recently had with another Western missionary. Unlike the learned Fr. Ma, this person looked much more like a wandering Daoist or Buddhist priest. He wandered among the common people preaching salvation to them. Moreover, if understood correctly, this particular Christian claimed that anyone who became a Christian would have to adjure the family rituals and sacrifices that held the Chinese world together. How could anyone teach such a barbaric doctrine? How could anyone argue against filial piety?

For a moment a frown crossed the face of Fr. Ma. He then composed himself and gave the following answer. Yes, this person was indeed another Christian priest from the West. Just as there were different schools of thought among the Confucians, say between followers of Master Zhu, or Master Wang, or of the new Evidential Research School, so too were there differences between and among different Christians. This other person was a priest in a different school. When pressed, Fr. Ma reluctantly admitted that there was something of a controversy between his school and the school of the other priest. It was true, alas, that the two schools differed on the nature of how to understand Chinese family ritual and devotions.

The Chinese scholars were shocked. How could there actually be any debate about something so simple, so elemental to good order and the true Way as the family rituals? Yes, Fr. Ma said, there were some fellow Christians who believed this (Franciscan missionaries), though his school (the Jesuits) rejected any such interpretation of Chinese family ritual. He went on to explain the origin of the problem. According to the teachings of the Lord of Heaven school, only the supreme god was worthy of worship. Although you could offer prayers to other saints and to the mother of god, only god could be actually worshipped as god. Some of this explanation made sense to Dr. Li and his friends. Confucians were conversant with certain forms of Daoism that had similar teachings about the role of spirits and gods or god. Some of these Daoist schools taught that you needed to understand the order of the heavenly hierarchy in order to achieve oneness with the Dao itself. But no Daoist would dare repudiate the family rituals that bound human beings together.

Fr. Ma went on to explain that the other school of Christians thought that the family rituals compromised their ban on worship of only the one supreme god. Of course, Fr. Ma spoke at great length about the fact that his school rejected this view as wrong. The research of Fr. Ma and his fellow priests showed that the Chinese family rituals were basically to remember and honor the family; in strict terms they were not worship per se. For instance, Fr. Ma said that it was fine for Christians to venerate the saintly people in the same way that Confucians venerated the memories of the great scholars of the past and their families.

The distinction that Fr. Ma made was between worship of the Lord of Heaven in a strict sense and the veneration of the ancestors as was common in Chinese culture. The conclusion of the Jesuit missionaries, after long consultation with Chinese scholars, was that, when properly interpreted, the ancestral rites were not worship but rather a form of civil veneration of the ancestors. If this were indeed the case, then it was entirely appropriate for the Chinese to continue with their family rites. There was only one other major fly in the ointment, and that had to do with the Christian view of marriage. The Christians demanded monogamy, which was not the Chinese custom. Chinese men were allowed to take more than one wife and even keep concubines. This was strictly forbidden by the Christian church and was another impediment for the conversion of many Confucians. Even if Confucians were convinced by the Christian preaching, most of them found it impossible to divorce their secondary wives. This would be a very unjust thing to do from the Confucian moral point of view.

Fr. Ma conceded that on the surface the other Christian missionaries had a point about the rites. The rites did seem a great deal like worship. In fact, many common people did believe that they worshiped their ancestors. However, as the Confucian scholars knew well, this was not the precise meaning of the family rites. This fine distinction between veneration and worship was lost on many Chinese and the other Christian missionaries as well. It was probably the most contentious issue in the whole debate about the Christian mission.

It was simply impossible for Confucians to conceive of giving up their family rites. One of the strongest of all Chinese moral virtues was filial piety. Around filial piety the Confucians had constructed an elaborate set of rituals for all occasions of life. One of the most important aspects of this was to offer thanks to the ancestors. It did not really matter if the family was "Confucian" or not. Family ritual was one of the great features of the Chinese religious and social world. No matter how humble the family was, there was always a shrine to the ancestors of the family. The most common focus was on the ancestor tablets, the wooden plaques upon which the names of the ancestors were lovingly engraved. To be without ancestors was to be without a self, to be a lost soul in the Chinese world. The more radical Christian missionaries wanted the Chinese to burn their family tablets upon becoming Christians. This struck the Confucians as insane.

The reason for this as the Confucians were told and Fr. Ma confirmed, was the belief of the other missionaries that only god was good. No human being was good. Of course, this teaching of human evil was in direct contradiction to the words of Mencius. Ever since the great Song revival the consensus was that Mencius was correct about the essential goodness of human nature. No Confucian scholar would say that this meant everyone would be good or would always act in a virtuous fashion. Our good nature was all too often obscured by a turbid endowment of vital force. This was why Confucians stressed the dual roles of self-cultivation and education. Only through real self-discipline could anyone hope to manifest the fundamental good nature. Nonetheless, it was a tenet of Confucian thought that human nature as principle endowed for each person from heaven was good.

To teach that human nature was evil was to fall into the mistake that Xunzi made so long ago. Moreover, there was another painful aspect of the new Christian teaching. Not only did it impute evil to the person, it also taught that the ancestors were sinful human beings. This was a step too far for Confucians to go. One might accept one's own corruption and need for all the moral help one could assemble, but it was unfilial to proclaim that the ancestors were wicked people in need of grace from a strange Western God. Fr. Ma was obviously not pleased to have to admit that this is what the other missionaries were teaching.

The immediate reaction of the Confucians was that if they had to give up filial piety, renounce the ancestral rites, adopt the view that human nature was evil, and even apply the human nature is evil doctrine to the ancestors, it would be impossible to be a good Christian and Confucian at the same time.

Plate 7 *This small building in an ancillary area in the Forest of Confucius is a typical Ming-style meeting and tea-drinking pavilion which might have been part of a scholar's study and garden.* Photo: Evelyn Berthrong.

7 FURNISHING THE STUDY AND HOSTING A READING

One of the things that every scholar dreamed of owning was a well-appointed study. This, of course, makes great sense because so much of the Confucian world revolved around education. It was in the study that the Confucian could commune with the ancient sages and worthies. A great deal of thought went into the planning for the ideal study. It was not just a place for books; it was also a place for art. It was here that calligraphy, poetry, and painting were perfected. It was here that music was played. It was a place that fantastic stones and small potted trees were appreciated for their beauty and cultural refinement. It housed the paper, brushes, and ink for the scholar to write his or her own poetry, histories, letters, or essays for family, friends, and a wider public.

It was a place to hang a painting or an example of fine calligraphy. Calligraphy and painting coexisted in a peaceful harmony, with strong influences going back and forth. However, they were considered separate art forms; not every great painter was a great calligrapher and vice versa. Along with the various forms of fine and decorative arts in the study, a view of the scenery was also an excellent feature. Of course, the kind of view possible from a window depended on the nature of the house. In an urban setting this could mean looking out at a courtyard garden, however modest it might be. A wealthy scholar could always choose to have a number of studies including a retreat far from the city in a forest, by a lake, or in the mountains, where the views would be magnificent.

Many Confucian scholars and their families loved to visit the country. The great Zhu Xi joked that it was hard to find a truly beauti-

146 ◆ Confucianism A SHORT INTRODUCTION

ful spot without a Buddhist monastery or a Daoist temple already built on it. There weren't enough places for a Confucian scholar to help build a temple much less their own studies in the midst of nature. Although Confucians have the reputation of being urbanites, many of them loved to travel in the countyside. They have even left a travel lore that reveled in mountains and wild places long before these scenes became fashionable in Europe.

Back in the city the study could also have many small plants, better known as bonsai in the Western world. If you could not go to the forest, you could bring the forest to you. Gardens were also an art for the Confucian scholar. In fact, Chinese gardens had a great impact on Europe during the Enlightenment period. The asymmetrical grace of the Chinese garden was a model for how human beings could interact with nature. In the house or study, the small bonsai themselves could be arranged as a garden in the urban setting.

STONES AND ROCKS

Another form of scholarly collection was fantastic stones and rocks and the name seals made from stone. The Chinese have always loved rocks and stones. Some of the earliest and most beautiful art objects we still have were carved out of jade even before the Shang dynasty. These early jades show the same kinds of artistic motifs that made the bronze vessels and objects of the Shang and Zhou dynasties so famous. The ancient bronzes had become so admired by the Song period that books were written about famous vessels and collections. Such books were needed because there was a flourishing forgery business in reproductions of Shang and Zhou bronzes. Remarkably by the Qing dynasty even some of the better Song forgeries were collected as antiques.

Dr. Li had just received a wonderful set of rocks from the far south as a gift from his father-in-law. The odder the rock, the more a Chinese scholar prized the specimen. Some of the rocks were just oddly formed; some of them looked like miniature mountains. Because Mrs. Li was skilled in growing bonsai, Dr. Li asked her to give special attention to one of the larger rocks. At first Dr. Li planned to put all the new rocks in the expanded garden around the new study, but he thought again when he saw one of the larger rocks.

This rock really looked like one of the strange, water-carved mountains from the south. Dr. Li would not have believed that real mountains could have looked like this unless he had visited that part of south China that was famous for its wondrously carved peaks. This was a tiny version of those peaks. It actually had three separate peaks, and wonderful little valleys and grottoes between the peaks. Mrs. Li agreed that this would be a wonderful addition to Dr. Li's older and smaller study. She would find various small plants that could be fitted into the gaps in the rock. In this way the rock itself would resemble the beautiful and dramatic topography of south China. It would bring refreshment to the mind of a scholar working on private or public business.

Another aspect of the building of the new study and laying out of the expanded garden was the choice of a *fengshui* or siting expert. Like any Chinese, Dr. Li would make use of the services of a *fengshui* expert when it came time to build any significant structure. Any house or tomb, for instance, demanded the services of someone skilled in this ancient and arcane art. The most common English translation for *fengshui* is geomancy. Although the most important aspect of geomancy was involved with finding the proper site for a tomb, it could also be employed for almost any other structure as well.

Fengshui was common to all classes of Chinese (and East Asian) people. The only other mantic art that matched its common usage was divination using the *Classic of Changes*. In times of stress or indecision, all classes of Chinese, including the most famous of Confucians, had recourse to casting a hexagram of the *Classic of Changes*. Although the connection of these two mantic arts may not appear obvious to a non-Confucian audience, there is a very important one. The connection resides in the abiding conviction, common to all forms of Chinese thought, that the world we perceive is one of interdependence of all things.

In the Confucian view, the world was a vast net or field of interlocking forces and events. Nothing happened in isolation from anything else. But there was a problem. Even though all was connected, all was not simple. Human beings had no innate or easy way to access knowledge of the various forms and processes of nature. The Confucian tradition tells of the origin of the *Classic of Changes* and of writing at the same time. The ancient primordial sage Fuxi invented both writing and the classic when he looked into the heavens and upon the earth to discover the "signs" of all things. Writing itself was a sign of how things really are, as are the trigrams (set of three solid or broken lines) and hexagrams (set of six solid or broken lines) of the *Classic of Changes*.

The *Classic of Changes*, though modern scholars no longer believe in the stories of the ancient sages, is one of the oldest of Chinese classics. At least parts of the classic are truly ancient; the only other work that goes back nearly as far may be some poems from the *Poetry Classic* and perhaps some materials in the *Classic of History*. The body of the *Classic of Changes* is not made up of Chinese graphs. The text is ordered around sixty-four hexagrams. This number is not random either. Sixty-four is the grand total of all the possible combinations between whole and broken lines. The hexagrams, and the sub-figures of the trigrams, are nothing more than combinations of solid, broken, or mixed figures of solid and broken lines. These lines, according to the legend of the invention of the *Changes* by the sage Fuxi, represent the basic patterns of the universe.

Along with the basic sixty-four hexagrams, there are layers of appended commentaries that were added to the basic text, purportedly, by other sages and worthies. These texts, rather gnomic in nature, were interpreted as clues to reading the situation at hand. In the later and longer appendages, known as the commentaries or the ten wings of the text, there is even a great deal of cosmological theory. The reason that someone like Dr. Li would consult the text was based on the theory that the text, when properly divined, could give direction when the person faced difficult decisions.

Of course, some Confucian scholars were not impressed with the mantic powers of the text. They preferred to read the classic as another example of the cosmological and moral teachings of the sages. Nonetheless, hallowed tradition suggested that the text meant something more than dry philosophy. It was a living link and voice to the thought of the sages – when properly consulted. For instance, Dr. Li would have known the engaging story of Master Zhu Xi's divination during a difficult political controversy in the twelfth century.

That Zhu Xi revered the *Classic of Changes* as part of the sage canon is undoubted. However, he seemed to have doubted some of the more mantic or magical uses to which the text was put. He allowed for divination, but of a restrained sort. Moreover, Master Zhu never let anyone forget that even divination was only useful when it was coupled with a heightened sense of moral cultivation, commitment, and practice. Zhu was worried that sometimes legitimate divination of the general and moral features of the cosmos might edge over into a false belief in numerology. The manipulation of the numerical values of the hexagrams in order to forecast the future, which was also part of the divination tradition linked to the *Classic of Changes*, verged on superstition from Zhu's viewpoint and ought not be part of a real Confucian's practice. However, with appropriate intellectual and moral hedges in place, divination could be helpful.

Furthermore, Master Zhu understood part of his role as a faithful minister to be willing, from time to time, to criticize the ruler when he believed the situation warranted such a reprimand. Although the Song dynasty was famous for its gentle treatment of high ministers, such an act was not without potential negative consequences. Political situations were not merely cosmic happenings; politics involved the interests and bickering of different parties. When someone as famous as Master Zhu took it upon himself to remonstrate via a written memorial to the emperor, this was serious business. It was doubly serious because it implied real criticism of the person and conduct of the emperor and, by extension, the policies of the court, including other high officials who disagreed with Zhu Xi's political stance.

Nonetheless, as the story goes, Master Zhu was resolved to write a lengthy and highly charged memorial to the throne. His students were afraid for the master. They did not believe that the memorial would change governmental policy. Moreover, the blunt memorial would only serve to irritate the emperor and anger the officials on the other side of the issue. Master Zhu debated the question of whether or not to send the memorial with his friends and disciples, but with no final outcome. It was suggested that this would be a perfect time to consult the *Classic of Changes*. The classic could be relied upon to give some direction to Master Zhu.

The method of divination was simple to begin with. Master Zhu would cast the hexagram; that is to say, he would make use of one of a variety of methods to build up his hexagrams of solid or broken lines until he had all eight. This would give him a specific hexagram. He would then consult the various written interpretations of the text. For a less learned person, the divined hexagram would be interpreted by a skilled expert in such lore. But Master Zhu had written commentaries of his own on the *Classic of Changes*, so he was more than able to read the answer for himself. The answer was emphatically negative. Against what had been his strong political and moral convictions, Master Zhu accepted the advice of his students and did not formally send the memorial. However, he did keep a copy that became part of his collected writings.

Actually, Dr. Li himself set about casting a hexagram in order to discover what would be a proper day to invite his good friend over to practice *fengshui* for his new garden and study. From the perspective of the two friends, *fengshui* and consulting the *Classic of Changes* belonged to the seamless web of the Dao. One, the hexagrams, is useful to selecting the right time for the second, the mantic art of *fengshui*. Both the hexagrams for time and the divination of siting work well together in the coordinated world of the five phases and the constant interaction of yin and yang, all governed by the creative power of the Supreme Ultimate.

Fengshui was another mantic art commonly used by Confucians and other Chinese. Its philosophic justification was similar to divination with the *Classic of Changes*. The major assumption underlying both divination and siting was the deep-set conviction that the world was an organic whole. Confucians, for instance, loved to speak of this unity via metaphors of plants. But the underlying assumption of the relational nature of reality did not depend on just one metaphor, even one as powerful for an agricultural society as the natural processes of plants. The ultimate aim of geomancy, like self-cultivation and medicine, was to maintain a balance of forces in an ever changing world.

One reason that Dr. Li was inclined to seek geomatic advice was that one of his very good friends was an expert in *fengshui*. Like medicine, geomancy was an accepted art and practice for a Confucian literati. As one would suspect, there were many competing forms of *fengshui*. Although all sought to harmonize human beings, their tombs, temples, and humble structures with the flow of the universe, different geomancers defended different methods.

Dr. Li's friend was from Fujian province and was learned in the special traditions of geomancy taught there. The Fujian tradition made extensive use of a geomantic compass. To call this large and wondrous device a compass does not do it justice. Cast in bronze, it is an iconic map of the cosmos itself. It includes not only a compass needle for telling directions, but also circles that will help to calculate time and relationships to the various five phases of the material world. In fact, the dial is engraved with the icons needed to divine the interrelationship of humanity with space, time, and the flux of the constant transformation of the cosmos. It has stars for astrology, symbols for the yin-yang forces and the eight basic trigrams, the nine prime stars, and so forth in great detail and beauty. The compass used by Dr. Li's friend had at least fourteen different dials that could be rotated while searching in the field for the correct placement of any object.

The potential complications were almost endless. The reason for this was the perennial Confucian conviction that the world was enormous and real; no one thing was precisely like another, and part of the difference lay in its spatial and temporal location. In this case, concerning the garden outside the study, one had to consider the interrelationship of the elements of water, wood, and earth (represented by the new rocks). This was a perfect example of the correlative nature of classical Confucian thought. Based on the theory of the five phases – fire, water, earth, wood, and metal – each and every item in the siting of the garden should be considered in relationship with each other. For instance, the placement of the artificial pond would help to determine the final placement of the new rocks. Dr. Li reflected, in the midst of his friend's calculations, that the old bronze compass itself was a true work of art, enfolding within its spheres and figurations the condensed wisdom of Confucian cosmological speculation.

Another question for Dr. Li was the choice of books and rubbings to place in the study. Books were an important part of a scholar's life, and Dr. Li had been assiduous since his youth in assembling a good collection. For the early part of his life he had mostly concentrated on collecting the essential works necessary for Confucian scholarship. This included, of course, the thirteen Confucian classics as well as many diverse commentaries on the texts themselves. The commentaries varied from very philological works that sought, in great detail, to explain every word and its usage to be found in the classic, to those that were more concerned with social and historical evolutions. Many, of course, were committed to a philosophic explication of the true meaning of the classics. Each kind of commentary was vital to the growth of a Confucian scholar. Along with the classics, there were independent philosophic, historical, and philological studies. All of these studies were supplemented by various specialized monographs, such as studies in mathematics, forensic medicine, and poetic theory. Another major set of books were the various famous anthologies of great works of the past and large encyclopedias that sought to organize the whole range of Chinese intellectual discourse.

Whereas some of these books were of a purely utilitarian nature, some were prized editions. Dr. Li had begun to scour the famous bookstores and publishing houses of Suzhou in search of early Song, Yuan, and Ming editions of famous works. Moreover, among these rare editions, there were some that had been printed in a beautiful font. In short, books themselves were art objects.

Dr. Li also wanted to display his small but cherished collection of rubbings. Over the centuries, different dynasties had commissioned the carving of the classics in stone. Scholars would visit the sites of these stone forests of learning and make rubbings directly from the stones. Another source of rubbings came from memorial reliquaries carved for famous scholars. Many of these reliquaries had famous inscriptions that were also prized for the words of former Confucian worthies. Needless to say, these rubbings were much larger, on the whole, than books. In fact, some of the rubbings could almost cover a small wall. They too reflected a scholar's taste and intellectual sophistication.

Two other kinds of objects also commanded Dr. Li's attention. The first set of treasures was ceramics. Mrs. Li, as befitting an educated daughter of a famous literati family, had many wonderful ceramics and insisted that he use some of them for the new study. Here again Dr. Li prized the older objects more than the new ones. Each dynasty had a different style. For instance, there was one strikingly beautiful horse from the Tang that demanded a special place in the study. It was large and done in refined yet bold colors, in which Dr. Li could sense the energy and splendor of a bygone culture.

The other ceramics he loved were from the Song dynasty. As a follower of Master Zhu, this was an obvious choice. Whereas the Tang horse was bold, the Song vases, bowls, and tea set were subtle. The clean, almost austere lines of these ceramics revealed their beauty. What always struck any connoisseur was the translucent quality of the glazes on even the most mundane Song objects. Somehow these refined objects fitted so well with the sober and sophisticated world of the Song philosophers. Their simple shapes and patterns reflected an attention to detail that matched the genius of their philosophic speculations.

The last item Dr. Li admired this day was his zither. The Chinese zither, which looked much like a modern Japanese koto, was an instrument of many strings. The various frets could be moved along the sounding board as the musician played the ancient airs and modern tunes. It looked like a simple instrument, but it was very difficult to play because it was so hard to keep in tune. Many scholars had zithers in their studies, but few could actually play them well. However, Dr. and Mrs. Li could both play well, though Mrs. Li was more accomplished, and they owned a number of zithers and enjoyed playing duets. Along with being a refined musical instrument, in fact, one of the constant companions of the Confucian scholar, a zither could also be a work of art. This one was inlaid with beautiful scrolls of mother-of-pearl and gold wire. Dr. Li was proud that his zither not only had a beautiful tone, but also was a remarkable piece of the artisan's skill. The zither would also need a special place in the décor of the new study.

A POETRY GATHERING

Educated Chinese women had always written and appreciated poetry. The oldest collection of Chinese poetry, the *Classic of Poetry*, includes many poems written from the perspective of women. Of course, the tradition taught that these poems were not really written by women at all, but by male poets who used a woman's viewpoint in order to make a specific impression. Among the poems in the *Classic of Poetry* are samples of the earliest writings we have from classical China. While some are political in nature, many are love poems speaking of the eternal longing of women and men for each other's company. The later scholarly tradition, shocked by the emotions expressed in the love poetry, developed elaborate theories to prove that the poems were actually political in nature and that the early love poetry was really just allegorical commentary on history.

By the Ming dynasty, probably because of the growth of sophisticated urban society and the expansion of commercial printing, we find more and more poetry written by women. This trend continued into the Qing and is unabated today. Whereas we have few poems by women from the earlier periods of Chinese history, we have a treasury of poems from the Ming and Qing periods.

Furthermore, in both Korea and Japan, women wrote works that have survived to the present. One reason for this was that both early and medieval Korea and Japan were highly aristocratic societies, and those sophisticated women had more freedom of life and expression than did their literati sisters in late imperial China. No one can forget the wonderful early Japanese novels or remain unmoved by the tale of a Korean princess's painful family saga, one that led to the death of her husband by starvation. Women in East Asia were certainly not without powerful voices. Poetry provided one important avenue for expressing the feminine view of reality.

In the late Ming (1560–1644) women formed poetry clubs. It was a venue for educated women to gather with other women who shared their fascination with poetry and the world of emotion and thought expressed in this genre. In the late Ming, the list of members of famous literary clubs could include all educated women: the wives, daughters, mothers, and grandmothers of the literati world as well as the educated courtesans of the pleasure quarters. So much for propriety when good poetry was to be written.

There is a wonderful story of a Ming viceroy returning to his home to find his august wife presiding over a famous poetry club that did indeed include the most famous courtesans of the day. When the rather flustered husband/official commented on the composition of the club, the wife remarked that since the wives and courtesans both had the same male clientele, why shouldn't these women also get together to write poetry? One would like to hear some of their other conversations as well, but these, decorously, have not come down to us.

By 1685 the social scene had changed once again. It would have been unthinkable for Mrs. Li to participate in a poetry gathering with educated courtesans. One of the effects of the Manchu conquest of China had been the reaffirmation of a more restricted view of the proper boundaries of female friendship. However, this coolness for publication of love poems from courtesans would not keep the women from discussing why this should be the case. Of course, there were women who believed that they should still be free to talk about love between the sexes.

The poetry club was meeting in Mrs. Li's private chambers. The women were having a heated debate about the role of emotions, especially erotic emotions, in the life of self-consciously Confucian literati women. This was actually a debate with an impeccable Confucian pedigree. It revolved around the role that emotions play in human life and their relationship to the deepest roots of human nature. In fact, the role of emotions in human nature was a key concern for the various schools of Confucianism.

One of the ways that Confucians distinguished themselves from Buddhists and Daoists was their acknowledgement of the reality of both human nature and the emotions. Although Buddhists and Daoists disagreed, the Confucians held that they alone had a realistic doctrine about human nature and emotions. If this were not the case, then why, the Confucians asked, did the Buddhists and Daoists spend so much time talking about the emptiness of all things and the void of the cosmos? Actually, more moderate Confucians understood perfectly well what the Buddhists and Daoists were talking about when they discoursed on emptiness (Buddhists) and the void (Daoists). What Buddhists and Daoists were really discussing was the fact that the world is a complex place in which we can never be sure that our emotions will not lead us astray because of inordinate self-interest. We are drawn towards self-interest; it might be better to free ourselves from emotions or void our conflicting and selfish motives, which are driven by our love of the pleasant and dislike of what is painful.

The Confucians accepted the need for restraint of misguided emotions but denied that this meant that the world was empty or void. The Confucians, including Mrs. Li, were wedded to a realistic and pluralistic view of the world. Moreover, Mrs. Li and her friends viewed the emotions as something valuable in and of themselves. The Confucian view was that emotions could be good or misguided depending on the circumstances. The question was not to try completely to eliminate feelings and emotions; rather, the true quest was to find the right way to engage the emotions. For instance, Confucius had said that it was appropriate to feel anger when confronted with social injustice. To be indifferent to injustice was to misunderstand the essential features of human nature in the Confucian reading of reality.

Some late Ming Confucian women made an even more interesting argument. It made use of some derogatory statements made by respected male Confucian philosophers about women. When asked why women could not be allowed to transact business beyond the "inner quarters", Master Zhu suggested that they were too emotional. The attribution of excessive emotionality seems to be a cross-cultural theme used to exclude women from fulfilling important public roles and responsibilities. In response, the Confucian women applied something like intellectual judo to Master Zhu's statement.

They accepted that Master Zhu was correct as far as he went; yes, because women were forbidden to have lives beyond the confines of their homes except for some occasional visits to homes of friends and temples, they did have a great deal of time on their hands to think about emotions. Moreover, the women also pointed out that because they did not have to undergo the arduous process of the examination system, this too allowed them to spend more time on artistic and emotional quests. However, while accepting that they were concerned with emotions, they noted that this did not diminish their intellectual capacities in the use of reason. There was a list of distinguished women who had contributed to the writing of history, poetry, and commentaries.

The key, the women went on, was whether or not women were educated. If they were allowed and encouraged to become educated women, then they could be the full intellectual equals of men. Moreover, the women argued that they would be better able to assist in their sons' education if daughters, wives, mothers, and grandmothers were educated. The argument was not always accepted, but many literati families did indeed provide education for their daughters. Many a Confucian father ruefully acknowledged the fact that he had a clever daughter and a dull son.

But the argument did not stop there. What kinds of emotions were proper for a literati woman to address? In theory, all emotions were subject to self-cultivation. The women asked, aren't the emotions generated by love between the sexes, even erotic feelings, especially important because they are so powerful? Because of an affirmative answer to this last question, many women poets in the late Ming believed that it was proper to explore fully the emotions of romantic love in light of their Confucian commitments.

Here the story of women, poetry, and the emotions became entangled with the history of Ming and Qing China. When the Ming dynasty was finally destroyed internally by civil wars and externally by the Manchu state, the Chinese elite asked the pointed question, why did the Ming fall? The question was exacerbated by the fact that the new dynasty was of non-Chinese origin. The Manchus worked very hard to play the role of a true Chinese imperial state, and they even produced some of the best emperors China had ever seen. But they were still a foreign conquest dynasty. During the early period of their rule, many Confucian literati refused to enter their service and pined for the old Ming dynasty.

But the question of why the Ming fell still remained. One answer given by Chinese intellectual historians was that there was a basic flaw in late Ming thought. It had become too expansive, too liberal, and in some cases, too libertine in nature. All of this talk about preaching to common people and cultivating all of the emotions bespoke not of real liberation, but of a social malady in the body of the country. What was needed was a return to more restrained values such as those found in the orthodoxy of the School of Principle. The School of Mind-heart, it was admitted, had produced many fine scholars such as Wang Yangming himself, but it had spawned irresponsible social activity as well. Too much emphasis on emotion was one mark of such social decay. The educated women of the Qing also thought about this question long and hard, and in the end, the women who published the great Qing anthologies of women's poetry abjured the more bold expression of emotion on the part of literati; including the works of educated courtesans, of course, was now completely out of the question.

But this whole issue of emotions was still a hot topic for debate in the poetry circle in which Mrs. Li moved. Just that afternoon her poetry club had read some of the Ming poems in question. The debate began when one woman shared a poem written in a popular style. Although no one was sure when it had been written, it spoke about the painful life of a courtesan at the lower end of the pleasure trade. It is a long poem, probably first set to music. It begins when the young woman is sold by her family into the life of prostitution.

> With all the sorrows of a prostitute,
>   I detest my parents:
>   Your greatest wrong
>   Was to sell me to the mist and flower lane;
>   Propriety, righteousness, honesty, and same
>   All mean nothing to you.
> At twelve and thirteen, I learned to play and sing;
>   Gradually growing up,
>   Groomed and displayed amidst the din of customers.
> I've a few dresses and a number of quilts,
>   Not to mention hairpins and makeup.
> When evening arrives,
>   In shame and misery,
>   I climb into the ivory bed;
> I steal a glance at the heartless cad:
>   Look at him!
>   In his whole being not a trace of elegance
> With no way to escape,
>   I am forced with him to enter the golden canopy;
>   Tossing and turning, he takes control of me.

The young courtesan continues to lament:

> I can never again
>   See my father and mother;
> Never again
>   Invite my own sisters into my room;

I can never
  Bear sons and raise daughters to keep the incense burning;
I can never
  Be famous as the elegant wife of a wealthy gentleman.
I have today
  Neither a surname nor a husband;
  My heart is empty, gloomy, and sad.
I have only
  A pair of jade-like arms to pillow a thousand men;
  And a pair of red lips to kiss ten thousand guests.
When I think of this,
  Tears well up in my eyes;
  This is worse than a life in Hell.
Filled with anxiety, I wonder,
  To whom will I belong in the future?
My cries must startle Heaven itself;
  Perhaps a former life has determined my present fate.
The only way out is this:
  To wait until one day there comes a man of feeling
  To rescue me with a decent marriage. (Widmer, 1997, pp.35–7)

At the other end of the scale, another woman read a poem by a famous later Ming courtesan, Liu Rushi. In this case Liu was much more upscale and even wrote poems back and forth to her literati guests, including her lover, Qian Qianyi.

Following the Same Rhyme, a Respectful Harmonizing

Under moon-lit curtains, as the songs subside,
  I search for the duster,
On the wind-swept bed, with books in disorder,
  I look for the hair-ornament.
The mist and water of the Five Lakes will always
  Be like this,
I wish to follow Zhiyi and drift along the swift stream. (Widmer, 1997, p.54.)

Here the lovers have been in Liu Rushi's boat. The boat and the water become metaphors for their place of love and the constantly changing vagaries of human emotion. Moreover, it turned out that Liu Rushi was no shrinking violet; she even once met Qian dressed as a man; along with her male disguise, Liu was also passionately interested in military history and affairs. Her self-image was often that of a *nuxia* or female knight-errant. Was there any wonder that a less adventuresome age would have problems fitting this brilliant courtesan into the pantheon of virtuous women poets? Qian Qianyi answered Liu Rushi's poems with his own.

> Heroes buried in the land of fragrant grass,
> Years worn away in the sky with setting sun,
> In the nuptial chamber, with the light of the autumn
>   lamp in the pure night,
> Together we studied the chapter "Discoursing on Swords"
>   in *Zhuangzi*. (Widmer, 1997, p.63)

It is not hard to see why such poetry was so challenging to Confucian ideals of female virtue. Here was a brilliant courtesan who lived as she pleased. Along with her genius for poetry, Liu Rushi was also an accomplished calligrapher and painter. Connoisseurs continued to appreciate her creations long after her death and the fall of the late Ming world she represented.

One of Liu Rushi's responses to Qian Qianyi sums up all the passionate commitment to romantic emotions perfectly.

> Harmonizing with the mysterious music of the goddess
>   of the River Xiang,
> Matching the Gourd with the Weaver Maid [both are names
>   of constellations]
> . . . .
> This [love] is not exhausted by those who seek
>   mere resemblance.
> How can it be fathomed by undiscerning communication? (Widmer, 1997, p.64)

Again Liu demonstrated her poetic genius and her classical education by alluding to famous mythological figures such as the goddess of the River Xiang as well as important constellations, which were also heavy with their own literary symbolism. It is not hard to see how a more sedate world would judge that things, that is to say romantic notions of love matches made in heaven, had gotten out of hand.

There was great debate in the club about whether or not this kind of emotional poetry was suitable fare. There was no doubt of its brilliance; rather, the question was about its emotional and moral level – was it possible to enjoy and write this kind of poetry from a Confucian perspective? One thing was affirmed by the members of the club, namely that there was nothing intrinsically wrong with emotions per se. In order to make this point, someone read another poem that expressed deep emotions in an altogether different direction.

Sitting in Silence

Sitting in silence, idly humming, I smile to myself,
Reaching the age of 69, I live in poverty.
From my tapestry loom pour elaborate new patterns,
From my giant inkstone roam tiny silverfish.
My family now has grandsons whom I teach to read,
Our house, though lacking in food, still keeps a library.
To satisfy one's wishes in a lifetime is a beautiful thing.
The vain world around me is mere emptiness (Mann, 1997, p.73)

There was immediate reaction to this poem. The first criticism was that it introduced a Buddhist note at the end. However, Mrs. Li pointed out that this was probably just a rhetorical flourish; besides, there was nothing wrong with using Buddhist insights to support the Confucian core of the poem. What was more Confucian, Mrs. Li urged, than a grandmother teaching her grandsons and providing a virtuous and learned example for her daughters and granddaughters? The emptiness here was merely a correct reading of the ethical situation. In straitened times one must remember that even the sages and worthies of antiquity taught that it was better to regard the gaudy pleasures of the world as vain and empty things rather than to obscure true virtue with a lust for material wealth. Besides, the family could not be that poor since they had managed to preserve their library.

Furthermore, there was nothing wrong with having some enjoyment in life as long as ultimate moral principles were kept in mind. Mrs. Li shared one of her favorite humorous poems, a poem re-written by a woman in imitation of a much more famous male poet of long ago.

In the Manner of Tao Qian

Living quietly, little to do
with the busy world,
it is my nature
to forget elaborate hairpins.
Green waters brim
in flower-scented pools,
cool winds are stored
in leafy woods.

Minnows play in wavelets and ripples,
wild birds sing out
their pleasing notes.
As evening comes
a timely rain,
white clouds deepen
on the highest peaks.
Plants in the yard are bathed
in nourishing moisture,
above mountain meadows
clouds send showers flying down.
Completely relaxed
I give thoughts free rein
to range far, far –
and when I like
pour for myself
some homemade wine. (Widmer, 1997, p.195)

From the perspective of the Chinese literary tradition, imitation was a mark of great respect, especially when it was done so cleverly.

At this point, one of the older women quoted a more didactic poem. Here again there was a long and honored tradition that allowed for a large place for poems of a highly didactic nature. Some of the earliest commentary on the *Book of Poetry* indicated that the major aim of poetry itself was to teach proper virtue through stimulating the emotions in the proper way. The poem ran like this:

Ban Zhao wrote the *Precepts for Women*,
that we might know the code of proper conduct.
I feel ashamed of my stupidity,
unable to correct my faults,
yet I pity those today who cultivate
appearances; they are only pretty dresses.
Not treating moral training seriously
will visit shame upon the family name.
Bring girls together, let them study,
teach them to distinguish right and wrong.
ask them to investigate essentials –
the Four Virtues, the Three Obediences –
make the ancient ways their standard. (Ko, 1994, p.164)

Given the seniority of the woman sharing the poem, all the other women agreed that it was a fine example of moral poetry. It urged women to study and to avoid frivolity. It demonstrated the place that Confucian education should have in the heart-minds of women.

This poem reminded someone of a woman of the period of the transition from the Ming to the Qing. Fang Weiyi and her younger sister were both widowed young; yet another sister took her own life in protest at the fall of her Ming dynasty. Although the two remaining Fang sisters did not have children of their own, they dedicated their lives to their own scholarship and writing as well as educating other children in their extended family. Fang Weiyi wrote the following suggestive lines of advice to a widowed niece with a young son to rear.

> Be steadfast like a rock.
> When your son completes his studies,
> Your day of honor and glory will come.
> Your unyielding integrity will shine in history,
> Generations will emulate your motherly virtue! (Ko, 1994, p.165–6)

All the assembled women agree that this was excellent advice. It was their role as Confucian women to teach the coming generations to embody the "unyielding integrity" that was the make of a just and righteous Confucian character. Although women lived their lives within the inner chambers, that did not discharge their obligation to education and moral cultivation.

Later generations of Chinese women criticize the classical, medieval, and early modern world that would not allow these talented women to play a role in the wider world. Nonetheless, the love of family and the dedication to education were not circumscribed, gender-limited aspirations. Perhaps the women were even more virtuous because they were forced to live in a limited world. However, one wonders if these highly educated women would not have bridled at the thought that they were not the mistresses of their own identities. Virtue, talent, and learning were the true mark of the person, and a woman could take pride in that her name would be revered for her wit, talent, and dedication to true virtue.

As the poetry club began to break up for the evening, Mrs. Li decided to seek some advice on an upcoming wedding for a favorite niece. She knew that her older friend was renowned, not only as a poet, but also as someone well-versed in ritual theory and practice. Mrs. Li had a problem. The difficulty was actually with the women in the family and not the men. As they had reviewed the plans for the wedding, it became clear that there was disagreement about how some of the rituals were to be performed.

Mrs. Li was born into a family that followed Master Zhu's collection of family rituals very closely. However, she discovered that not everyone did so, and that in fact there were even different versions of Master Zhu's famous ritual text that added or changed some aspects of the wedding ritual. This bothered Mrs. Li, so she raised the question with her friend.

The friend agreed that proper ritual was important. However, she went on to point out that Master Zhu himself, in following the teachings of his own masters, had combined and even transformed some of the rituals he recorded in his book. The argument was simply that each ritual had its fundamental intent and that some modifications due to season and geography might well be in order. For instance, the kinds of clothes mentioned for a wedding in the far north of China in the middle of winter would not make very much sense for a marriage in the south of China during a very hot summer. In fact, wearing certain kinds of clothes could cause the bride to faint dead away.

Therefore, even the great Zhu Xi had believed that it was possible to modify, as Confucius had done before, certain minor details of the ritual ceremony. Of course, the major elements should be observed properly. When Mrs. Li shared the debate within the family with her friend, her friend asked Mrs. Li how she would rate the change in terms of minor or major. Was it a major deviation to place different members of the family in a different place for the ceremony? And how would one decide what the correct answer to this question was?

Mrs. Li immediately saw the logic of her friend's counsel. For instance, if the change suggested was to disorder the generations, that is to say, if it was not to respect the place of the older members of the family, then this clearly was a major question. However, if the change was merely between aunts of the same generation, then this was a much more minor matter. Because the debate in Mrs. Li's family was about the place of members of the same generation and relationship to the niece, this was more a minor question than a major one.

The friend nodded her agreement. She went on to point out that there were many different editions of Master Zhu's *Family Rituals* due to regional variations or local customs. Where a family had a long and scholarly tradition of its own, and if the changes were minor, then it was really proper to follow the tradition of the family rather than the letter of the law from Master Zhu. This explained why there was sometimes honest disagreement on the precise nature of a wedding or some other ritual. The important thing was to preserve the spirit and main structure of the ritual. Because of this conversation, Mrs. Li decided to side with those who were seeking to follow the tradition of their own family.

Plate 8. *Performers in Manchu dress present an elaborate welcoming ritual loosely based on descriptions of Confucian ceremonies at the Confucian Temple in Qufu. The 2550th anniversary of Confucius' birth was celebrated in 1999 and an international symposium of Confucianism was held in Beijing and Qufu to mark the occasion. Coincidentally, 1999 was also the 50th year of Chinese communist rule. Photo: Evelyn Berthrong.*

8 INTO THE GLOBAL AND MODERN WORLD

We have spent most of our time introducing Confucianism set in the year 1685 with our invented, prototypical and idealized Confucian couple, Dr. and Mrs. Li. It is now time to move outward in space and forward in time. Confucianism, especially since the fourteenth century, became a truly international movement. Although most people think of Confucianism as quintessentially Chinese, this is no longer true.

INTERNATIONALIZATION OF CONFUCIANISM

Very early on in the formation of the East Asian cultural world, Confucianism spread to Korea, Vietnam, and Japan as part of the Chinese culture that was so much admired throughout the region. If early foundation myths and legends are to be believed, it arrived very early on the scene in Korea.

The Korean legend goes like this. When the Shang dynasty was replaced by the Zhou because of the infamous iniquities of the last Shang king, a high official from the new Zhou dynasty was dispatched to rule over what would later become the northern part of Korea. Therefore, later Koreans could and did claim that their country inherited the mantle of Zhou enfeoffment from its very inception. Scholars have learned to be doubtful about such legends, yet modern archaeology has tended to confirm some of these early stories. Whether or not some Zhou dynasty prince or duke was really sent to Korea and whether or not he really established a Chinese-style rule is not the point. The fact is that later Koreans saw this story as making them part of the larger history of Confucian East Asia.

At the other end of the emerging Chinese world, in the far south, Vietnam was actually part of the Chinese empire for hundreds of years. In fact, the Han dynasty included the northern parts of modern Vietnam in its imperial state. The Chinese controlled part of Vietnam off and on until well into the Ming dynasty, when the Chinese finally decided that it was not worth the military effort to keep the Vietnamese in the Chinese empire. The Vietnamese had made it perfectly clear by means of successful revolts against their Chinese overlords that they definitely did not want to be another province of China.

This did not mean that the Vietnamese were not enthralled by the spectacle of Chinese culture. They also imported and developed their own brand of Confucianism along with other aspects of Chinese civilization. However, unlike the cases of Korea and Japan, we know comparatively little about the development of Confucian thought in Vietnam. The original texts in Chinese and Vietnamese still exist, but they have not received much scholarly attention from either Western or Vietnamese researchers. The story of the Vietnamese transformation of Confucianism is still to be told.

It is an important story because Vietnam has straddled the divide between East and South Asian cultures for centuries. Vietnam, in the north of what is now called Indo-China, has been part of the East Asian world. But as the Vietnamese people moved into the southern parts of their country, the Vietnamese were in constant contact with people and states who derived their high cultural traditions from India. Just like the Vietnamese language itself, Vietnamese culture is a rich combination of Chinese and Indian elements. The Vietnamese experience, no doubt, will throw light on how the great exported cultures of China and India interacted over the centuries.

KOREA

The main developments of Confucianism outside China, according to modern scholarship, took place in Korea and Japan. Korea, as in so many other cases, was the transmitter of Chinese culture to Japan. While Japan and China later established their own commercial, cultural, and diplomatic relations, much of what the Japanese learned about China was mediated via Korea, during the formative years of the Japanese state. This makes a great deal of sense because many critical modern scholars believe that the ancestors of the modern Japanese people arrived in Japan from Korea. There has always been a close, though often tense, relationship between these two countries. The various wars, and later the Japanese conquest and colonization of Korea, have tended to make both sides wary of recognizing the closeness of the two peoples.

For instance, modern linguistics has theorized that Korean and Japanese both belong to the same language family. They are the most eastern extensions of the great Ural-Altaic language group that runs from Japan to Finland – the largest single sub-family of languages in the group would be the Turkish speaking people of central Asia. Mongolian and Manchu are also related languages. This fact has often been overlooked because the Koreans and Japanese both adopted literary Chinese as the medium of higher learning. It was not till the early modern and modern period that scholarship was commonly written in either Korean or Japanese.

Along with their political and military contests over the centuries, both Korea and Japan developed societies radically different from each other and from China. One of the key points of difference was the role that Confucianism played in the traditional lives of the Korean and Japanese people. For instance, it is fair to say that although Confucianism was well known in both countries from the medieval period on, it did not play a major role in the lives of the Koreans and Japanese until much later. Confucianism had been declared the official state orthodoxy in China as far back as the early Han period. However, Confucianism did not become the orthodox teaching in Korea till after the founding of the Choson dynasty in 1392. In Japan, Confucianism never became the orthodox teaching at all. It was only part of the ruling ideology of the Tokugawa government after 1600.

Along with the different receptions of Confucian studies in Korea and Japan, there was the fact that Korea and Japan had radically different forms of social organization. Both countries in contrast to China after the eleventh century, remained highly aristocratic societies. For instance, even though the Koreans adopted the Confucian-inspired examination system after 1392, the examinations were only open to a small fraction of the male population. Even the sons of elite fathers by concubines could not sit for the examinations. Slavery also continued to exist in Korea long after it had been abolished in China. Korea remained a highly stratified society. Confucianism became the state orthodoxy, but only members of the *yangban* aristocracy (the hereditary clans that controlled Korea during the Confucian era) could be full-fledged members of the ruling elite.

Prior to 1392 many Korean scholars had taken a deep interest in Confucian studies, but the primary place in the society was dominated by the highly articulate and developed Buddhist community. As was the case later in Japan, the learned monks were often Confucian scholars as well. However, the official position of Confucianism changed dramatically in 1392 with the foundation of the Choson dynasty. This dynasty would reign until it was abolished by the Japanese in 1910 when they conquered Korea as part of the Imperial Japanese Empire. Choson Korea was the longest lasting Confucian dynasty in East Asia. The young king and his advisors in 1392 decided that they would make Confucianism the state ideology of their new dynasty.

Moreover, the new Choson dynasty did not merely adopt Confucianism per se, they specifically established Zhu Xi's school of principle as the arbiter of orthodox doctrine and practice. The intellectual and social saga that followed on the choice of Zhu's school of principle was unparalleled even in East Asia. For instance, though Korean scholars would learn of the other Chinese schools of Confucianism, they remained staunch partisans for Master Zhu. Unlike in China or Japan, there was no effective challenge to the power of Zhu's vision till the fall of the dynasty. All Korean scholars were expected to study Zhu's thought in order to take the all-important state examinations.

The social or practical side of the coin is equally fascinating. Korea became the self-proclaimed most Confucian country of all East Asia, and was proud of the fact. Especially after 1644 when the Chinese Ming dynasty fell to the Manchu Qing dynasty, the Koreans claimed that they alone of all the states in East Asia should be considered an orthodox Confucian state. There was merit to their claim. The Koreans labored assiduously not only to master the intricate teachings of the school of principle, but also to practice the Confucian Way in ritual and everyday life.

For instance, no one followed Master Zhu's *Family Ritual* in all aspects of life as assiduously as the Koreans. As we have seen in our study of Chinese ritual theory, many Chinese scholars felt completely justified in modifying Master Zhu's teachings on the basis of their own scholarship or in the name of hallowed local or family custom. This was not the case in Korea. Even though Korean social custom was not overly Confucian in 1392, the Choson court and the *yangban* classes made every effort to follow Zhu's prescriptions to the very letter.

One of the most interesting outcomes of this search for a proper fusion of theory and practice was played out in the marriage ritual. The Koreans set about making Zhu's theory of marriage ritual the norm for all society. This caused some rather drastic changes in previous Korean marriage customs. The Korean aristocratic women were generally more socially active than their literati Chinese sisters – though it should be noted that both Korean and Chinese women, at least in theory, had more rights than did Western women in the medieval and early modern world.

Anthropologists argue that the most difficult to change and most enduring social customs of any society are its marriage and food customs. Even long after a transformation of language, people will continue ancient marriage and food rituals. The Koreans kept their distinctive cuisine but modified their marriage patterns to conform to Zhu's ideal pattern. No one followed Zhu more closely than did the Koreans after 1392. Questions of inheritance, lineage rights, the position of widows, and many other parts of the customs of marriage were transformed to fit the perfect Chinese model. In their love of Confucian ritual, the Koreans could and did make the strong case that they were more Confucian than the Chinese.

In the sphere of philosophic ideas, the Koreans first learned and then creatively adapted Confucian philosophy. The most well known case of Korean creativity is embedded in the famous "four-seven" debates in the sixteenth century. The nature of the debate is not obvious in the name "four-seven." The term comes from two different sets of emotions found in the classics. One list has four items and the second lists seven different emotions. The presenting question was then, how do these two divergent lists tally with each other?

The basic assumption behind the debate is that there had to be some rational way to explain why the ancient sages had provided two separate lists of the emotions. All the debaters actually agreed that there was such a reason, a theory that was derived from the philosophy of Zhu Xi and the other Song Confucian masters. The distinction of the four and seven, it was believed, rested on the differentiation of the emotions into two separate states of the human mind-heart. The first state was called "prior," and the second was "posterior." This meant that when we view our emotions "prior" to stimulation via the senses through contact with the things and events of the world, we can see their essential structure prior to the intervention of forces beyond the very structure of the emotions themselves. But after contact with the world, we then have another set of emotions, in this case the seven emotions of the second list.

But the presenting question still remains, namely, how are these two sets of emotions to be correlated with each other? The philosophic answer to this question was derived from another set of Master Zhu's teaching. Master Zhu, as we have already seen, argued that there was an ideal state, the state of principle, which was always embodied in vital force, the active, concrete world of things, events, and people. The essential was to be found in principle, but its manifestation could vary according to the allotment of vital force given to every person at birth. Hence human nature as principle was essentially the same for everyone, but the vital force was different, allowing for divergence of human outcomes in the concrete world. The Confucian scholars then argued that the "prior" list of four emotions were to be identified with principle whereas the seven later emotions were stimulated within the dynamic world of vital force.

Again, this was a reading of the primary classical texts that was not disputed within the "four-seven" debate. However, the Korean scholars sensed that there was an even deeper problem with this formulation, notwithstanding its apparent agreement with Master Zhu. The problem was with the nature of principle itself. In a nutshell, the Korean scholars asked, how can the living reality of vital force be governed or determined by abstract principle understood as the formal principle of each thing? Or as one famous Chinese scholar put it, how can a dead principle ride upon the living horse of vital force? Moreover, the seemingly fundamental separation of principle and vital force, although present in some writings of Master Zhu, went against other strong statements by the Song philosopher. Whenever a student asked if principle and vital force were separate substances, Master Zhu answered that it was crystal clear that principle and vital force were everywhere and always inseparably linked in all things, events, and persons.

The debate took many turns, but one of the most fascinating aspects was to ask a refined version of the question, what is the nature of principle? Is principle merely a dead pattern or does it contain the seeds to vitality within it? What was particularly pertinent about the debate is that it addressed, or rather expanded, an area of speculation that had been inconclusively addressed by the great Zhu Xi. Although we will not follow the twists and turns of the debate, it is certain that the Korean scholars involved achieved a new level of sophistication in their questions and answers. Even at the end of the debate, they were still looking to further clarify the underlying issues. The Korean scholars not only modified marriage arrangements, but also extended the range of Confucian philosophy.

The debate extended over two generations. Moreoever, it was a debate carried on with utter sincerity, passion, clarity, and universal goodwill. It never occurred to the participants to argue that their partners in debate were not good Confucians. All the participants assumed that they were Confucians seeking a better understanding of the relation of human emotion to ethical principle. Moreover, they did not pull any intellectual punches. When they thought each other wrong, they would so argue, but always with charity driven by the common conviction that many minds working together were better than one.

Although this was an intellectual debate about essential features of the Neo-Confucian worldview, it was also a discussion with a spiritual dimension. One of the points of the debate was to clarify what was meant by each list of emotions. As we recall, one of these lists was characterized as "prior" to contact with the common world of things, events, and persons. Much of the debate revolved around how to understand the terms of the question in relation to the classical texts and their Neo-Confucian commentaries. However, there was also an experiential tone to the query of the debate. The query was, is it possible to experience the four "prior" emotions when so much of human life depends on contact with the world? In fact, doesn't "experience" mean experience of something that resides beyond the mind-heart of the individual person?

The great Korean Confucians were convinced that they needed not only to understand or analyze the philosophic deposition of Master Zhu, but also to embody it in their lives. Here philosophy edges over into what is considered a religious quest in Western terms. However, it is better to think of the Confucian vision as a unified way of life. Of course, the great philosophers such as Zhu Xi, and his Korean disciples such as Li T'oegye (1501–70) and Li Yulgok (1536–84), the stalwarts of the "four-seven" debates, understood very well the distinction between analysis and spiritual discernment. Nonetheless, these Confucians stoutly maintained that analysis and spiritual discernment were part of a continuum of reflection and action and not two hermetically separated forms of life. There was one form of life, and it had many dimensions.

In terms of the cultivation of the mind-heart, both the states of prior to contact and after contact with things, events, and persons were vital to the progress of Confucian self-cultivation. This was a living and relational process of self-cultivation. This affirmation of the unity of the intellectual and spiritual life is one of the reasons that the Korean scholars worried so much about the nature of principle. They saw the world as alive, and this must therefore include principle as the normative element of human nature. Nothing could be "mere" or "pure" reason or principle in the sense of indifference to an ethical life.

JAPAN

As we mentioned briefly above, the Japanese case was different from that of both Korea and China. The most salient point to notice is that Confucianism became a vital force in Japanese life rather later than the other great Chinese ethico-religious import, Buddhism. From the scanty records we have of the very early period of Japanese history, knowledge of Confucianism was transmitted to the islands by scholars from the Korean peninsula. By the time the first Chinese-style state was being established in the sixth and seventh centuries, Confucianism was a part of Japanese life, albeit in a fairly minor way. However, the very first Japanese "constitution" of Prince Shotoku, promulgated in 604, contained mostly Confucian admonitions. This made sense even early on to the Japanese because Confucianism was always recognized as having the edge over Buddhism in terms of civil administration.

It was not until centuries later, with the founding of the Tokugawa shogunate in 1600, that Confucianism commenced to play a major role in Japanese life. Prior to that time Confucianism, though studied as part of the Chinese cultural legacy, was much less important than Buddhism. The main intellectual and religious energies of the Japanese elite were concentrated on Buddhism and the creation of unique and powerful new Japanese schools, such as Zen and Pure Land. Moreover, the Japanese preserved, as living forms, many classical schools of Buddhism that had disappeared in China and even Korea. The Buddhist monasteries often became schools for the clerical and lay elite, and Confucianism was part of their curriculum. Although Confucianism did not play a major role in the intellectual life of Japan, Japanese scholar-monks kept an eye on the developments of Confucian thought in China and continued to collect and cherish Chinese books. For instance, Song Neo-Confucian thought was introduced into Japan not long after it had been developed in China – but again, it did not flourish till much later.

However, with the founding of the new Tokugawa regime (1600), things changed and Confucianism emerged from the shadows of

Buddhist patronage. We need to review the nature of this new Japanese government. First, it is vital to remember that the Japanese term for the Tokugawa overlord was *shogun*. The shogun was not an emperor or a king; technically speaking, the shogun was the chief military leader of the Japanese empire. What was the relation of the shogun to the Japanese emperor? The emperor reigned but did not rule and continued to live in the ancient capital and cultural center of Kyoto. Theoretically the shogun ruled in the name of the emperor, though all effective power was in the hands of the shogun and the shogun's agents, including his representative stationed in Kyoto.

The Tokugawa shoguns believed that they needed to devise a new ruling ideology for their government. They reasoned that the older justifications for the shogunate had failed; the reason for the failure was clear to everyone. Until the Tokugawa family reunited Japan, the previous period had been a miasma of unbridled military conflict. The Tokugawa were adamant that they would bring peace and harmony once again to Japan. In terms of power relations, the Tokugawa made sure that they appointed members of their own family or strong supporters to crucial and large feudal domains. Although the Tokugawa allowed some of their strongest enemies to retain their territories, mostly in the southern part of Japan, they always made sure that the Tokugawa clan maintained overwhelming military power.

During the wars of reunification that led to the formation of the Tokugawa shogunate, not all the battles were with other feudal lords. Some of the most intense battles were fought with various militarized Buddhist sects. Although it may seem odd to the outsider, many Japanese Buddhist temples and sects maintained their own armies of warrior-monks for defense of their lands and interests during the period of civil turmoil prior to the Tokugawa reunification. Having tasted secular power, many militarized Buddhist leaders did not want to renounce the power that they had won in battles with other feudal lords. Because of the living memory of this armed conflict with the militant wing of Japanese Buddhism, the Tokugawa shoguns were loath to rely on Buddhism as a unifying ideology for their new state.

The other obvious candidate for an ideology of state formation was Confucianism. It was a very appealing option, and was enthusiastically embraced by the early Tokugawa rulers. They realized that Confucianism was just the kind of ideology that would help them create a stable new government. However, it is important to note that the Tokugawa rulers did not rely exclusively on Confucianism for their ruling ideology. They were well aware that Japan was a different country from China and that they could not replicate all the features of a Neo-Confucian Chinese state.

Moreover, the Tokugawa shoguns had no actual desire to Confucianize Japan in the same way the Choson dynasty in Korea had decided to do previously. The Tokugawa were military men and understood that they could not retain the loyalty of their feudal retainers, the samurai, if they tried to impose a purely civilian ethos. They needed to temper their newfound respect for Confucianism with a place for samurai's self-worth. The Tokugawa were highly successful in establishing such a synthesis with Confucianism as a major component of the system. The Tokugawa ruled Japan until their regime was replaced by the Meiji Restoration (which restored direct rule, theoretically, of the Japanese Emperor) in 1868. The fall of the Tokugawa, by the way, had more to do with the opening of Japan to the Western powers after the arrival of an American fleet in 1853 than with any overwhelming internal problems.

There were many unique features of Japanese society that shaped its creative acceptance of Confucianism. One of the most interesting examples has to do with the place of Confucianism in a feudal society where loyalty to the feudal lord is perceived as the highest possible human virtue. We have already discovered that in the Chinese world, loyalty was to the immediate family and not to the government. Moreover, China after the Han dynasty no longer had a completely feudal society in the same sense that Japan did.

One of the things that Japanese Confucians accepted was loyalty to their particular feudal lord, next to the shogun, and finally to the emperor. Another distinctive feature of the Japanese ordering of society was the belief that the emperor was of divine origin. Unlike the Chinese and Korean dynasties that came and went with regularity, the Japanese state myth taught that the Japanese imperial family was descended from the founding gods of the Japanese land. Loyalty was reinforced by a religious understanding of the chain of command from the emperor to the shogun, from the shogun to the feudal lords, from the feudal lords to the samurai, and from the hereditary and aristocratic national local government to the common people.

One of the outcomes of the Japanese retention of their feudal form of government was that the ideal of a universal examination system was never instituted in Japan. No careers were open to talent. In fact, one of the things that the Tokugawa decreed was that there was to be no mixing of the elite, that is to say, from the samurai on up, with the common people. Birth determined one's place in Japanese society. There might be examinations, but they were only for the samurai elite. Government service, as in Korea, was open only to the aristocrats.

Oddly enough, this lack of a comprehensive and universal examination system provoked a great burst of creativity in the development of Japanese Confucianism in the seventeenth and eighteenth centuries. The Japanese Confucians were feudal retainers in the employ of their respected domain lords, known as the daimyo. This employment via patronage rather than success in a standardized examination system allowed the Japanese thinkers to follow their intellectual inclinations. For instance there were flourishing schools that followed the thought of Wang Yangming rather than Zhu Xi's orthodoxy. This would not have happened in Korea.

Because of the particular moral demands of the feudal system – we have already noted the importance of loyalty to one's lord – many Japanese Confucians were acutely aware that their social system diverged greatly from either Chinese or Korean models. Some Confucians argued for a Confucian universalism because the same heaven's mandate covered Japan as well as China. Although there was room for regional differences in social customs, the essential features of Confucianism should hold in any country.

Other Confucian scholars were much more impressed with the Japanese historical experience and devoted themselves to studying the Japanese past. This led to a reaction against the universal claims of Confucianism with its specification of Chinese culture as the norm. For example, some nativist scholars argued that Japan had a better political system because it was based on the divine fact of the imperial house. The Japanese emperor was divine and not merely human as was the case in China (or Korea). In fact, it was during the rise of Confucianism in the Tokugawa period that there was also an increase in purely Japanese studies. Although these Japanese studies were often linked to a renewed fascination and appreciation of Shinto spirituality, many Confucians firmly believed that they could revere the Shinto *kami* or spirits as well as function as Confucian scholars.

Another Japanese development was the founding of Confucian schools for the increasingly wealthy merchant families around the great city of Edo (modern Tokyo) and other flourishing urban centers. One of the unanticipated outcomes of the Tokugawa success was the growth of large cities and the rise of a sophisticated national economic network. Because samurai were not supposed to sully their hands with commercial activity, greater and greater power fell into an emerging business elite. In order to provide education for their sons and employees, the great merchant trading and banking houses established their own Confucian academies. These academies provided a solid Confucian (and business) education to the scions of commerce. They took their Confucian studies seriously, and there was even sustained conversation between this class of merchant Confucian scholars and the samurai elite. Both shared a common veneration for the fundamentals of a Confucian worldview.

In the world of the common people, there was a movement of Confucian local preachers who taught in Japanese. They even composed popular hymns and wrote children's books to bring the essentials of Confucian learning to the Japanese farmers and poorer urban and village people. They devised forms of social organization in the eighteenth century that bore an uncanny resemblance to the social organization of the Methodist movement in England by John Wesley. Both Wesley and Teshima Toan (1718–86) believed that the common people had been deprived of proper ethical and spiritual nurture. Both men developed small classes of study for their followers in order to introduce them to Christianity and Confucianism, respectively. Confucianism, which had previously been confined to the samurai world, was spread much more broadly into the fabric of Japanese society at all class levels.

There was also a burst of philosophic activity among the Japanese Confucians. There was, for instance, a strong empirical bent to the work of thinkers such as Kaibara Ekken. Although Ekken perceived himself as the follower of Zhu Xi, he developed a novel approach to some key philosophic terms. For instance, he believed that principle as the Supreme Ultimate was really a formal name for the primordial vital force. Ekken also believed in the power to doubt. In fact, he argued that doubts must be used to extend the range of studies.

In short, both philosophically and socially, the Tokugawa Confucians were highly innovative. These Japanese Confucian scholars demonstrated, as did the Koreans and Vietnamese, that Confucianism had become a truly transnational movement. In fact, we can make the argument that one of the outcomes of the modern transformation of the

Confucian world in East Asia is that Confucianism has now begun to move outward into the broad global city of the new century and millennium.

INTO THE MODERN WORLD

Many traits from the early modern period in East Asia are still manifested in contemporary Confucianism in East Asia. However, for a time in the early part of the twentieth century it did appear that Confucianism was a dead tradition for all practical purposes. Vietnam had become a French colony and Korea had been annexed by Japan. Japan, in its eager search for wealth, power, and international prestige, sought to distance itself from the partially Confucian ideology of the Tokugawa era. The great success of the Meiji Restoration obscured the continuing nature of Confucianism's impact on Japanese life. In China, the 1911 revolution swept away the ancient Chinese empire and all of its official Confucian trappings. The order of the day appeared to be a thorough and rapid Westernization of East Asia. Clearly Confucianism was not to play a role in the modernization of East Asia.

The early effort toward modernization was always linked to some form of Westernization. In the case of Japan, the first and still most successful practitioner of rapid modernization, this meant the selective borrowing of various features of Western culture. For instance, the Japanese invited the English to assist them in founding the Imperial Japanese Navy at the same time they were inviting Germans to reform the Japanese army. Various French and American experts were also brought in to work on industry, medicine, politics, and cultural matters. However, after the first flush of complete Westernization, the Japanese realized that modernization was possible based on a selective borrowing of Western technologies without abandoning all of traditional Japanese culture. For instance, the Meiji period saw the reformation of Buddhism and Shinto, in terms both of study and practice.

Confucianism suffered a particular problem in East Asia because it was so closely identified with the ancient regime. If Confucianism was the main cultural element of East Asian culture, and if East Asia was so far behind the West in terms of wealth and power, then Confucianism must be to blame for this failure. One solution to this problem was to expunge Confucianism as a living tradition. It will be noted that the religious or spiritual dimension of the rush to modernization did not include a "Westernization" of religion. Although a massive and sustained Christian missionary movement was launched in East Asia, East Asians did not flock to convert to Christianity as eagerly as they converted to the other two twins of modernization, science and democracy. Of course, there were exceptions to this rule, with Korea and the Philippines developing large Christian communities.

There are a number of reasons for this more traditional attitude towards matters spiritual. The first is that religious beliefs are conservative in nature. The conservatism takes different forms and should not be too readily linked to a reactionary view of reality. The New Confucians are conservators of the Confucian tradition but they are also harsh critics of previous forms of thought and practice as well as reformers of all aspects of the tradition. They reform that which they seek to preserve. The New Confucians do so because they argue that there is something intrinsically laudable about Confucianism. The same argument was used during the Meiji reform about various aspects of traditional Japanese culture.

The pragmatic strategy deployed in East Asia when intellectuals began to grapple with the question of modernization, made use of a very traditional Confucian device. This was the theory of essence and function. The argument was that every culture, just like every object, event, or person, has both essential and functional features. The essential features define who and what we are, but the functional features activate these essential features in distinctive ways. The idea was to keep Confucian culture as the essence of the civilization while using Western technologies to make the country strong and wealthy. Therefore, it was completely appropriate to use Western science and technology in support of Confucian ethical norms.

This argument about Eastern values and Western science and technology (democracy was viewed as a modern political technology) was articulated at more or less the same time in China and Japan, but with dramatically different results. The Japanese, to begin with, were much more willing and eager to embrace a much greater dose of radical or total Westernization as part of the process of modernization. However, the Japanese quickly realized that it was not that easy to separate essence from function.

A perfect example would be in the area of spiritual values and praxis. Could one, for instance, become modern and "Western" without becoming Christian? The Japanese made the decision, both individually and as a society, that one did not need to convert to Christianity in order to make use of other Western forms of modernization. But Japanese intellectuals did discover that modernization would and did change traditional forms of spiritual and religious life along with everything else it touched. Modernization had an impetus of its own.

The Chinese experience was less successful. The Chinese fell farther and farther behind the Japanese, to the point that the Chinese were defeated decisively in the Sino-Japanese War of 1895. This was a shock to the Chinese system. It was at this point that many Chinese began to question whether or not it was possible simply to graft Western technology onto the old Chinese cultural system. Increasing numbers of Chinese intellectuals came to the conclusion that the problem of modernization would defy an "easy fix" in the sense that the essence and function could not be simplistically separated. They reasoned that Western culture and technology was a fairly unified package, and that in order to embrace the powerful new technologies, many major modifications would have to be made to Chinese culture.

One strong suggestion was that China model itself on the most progressive aspects of Western culture. This was an argument that was used, for instance, against both Confucianism and Christianity. Thus, even though Christianity was a basic element of Western culture, it was only a formative element, playing a reduced role in modern life. In fact, so the argument went, religion was on the wane in the West. Therefore, if China wanted to modernize as quickly and effectively as possible, it should adopt the most "modern" form of Western culture. The radical intellectuals of early twentieth century China did not believe that Christianity or Confucianism would fit well into a modern China. The real debate was whether China should follow a liberal, pragmatic, democratic path of reform or embrace a more radical leap into modernity as promised by the communist movement. As everyone knows, after a terrible half century of despair, civil war, foreign attacks, and finally the massive Japanese invasion in the Second World War and the great civil war that led to the formation of the People's Republic of China in 1949, China chose the most radical method of modernization possible from the Western inventory, namely the revolutionary method of the communist party.

Yet, at the time when the West was perceived to be most powerful, many East Asian intellectuals were shocked by the savage nature of the First World War. If Western culture was so advanced, why was it unable to restrain the carnage of the Great War? There was suddenly a renewed interest in the humane and spiritual values of the great Asian traditions. Perhaps there was something worth saving from the onslaught of modernization and Westernization.

It was out of the hope for the reformation of Confucian philosophy and culture that the New Confucian movement was born in China. However, the decades of civil war and then the Second World War, followed by another civil war, ultimately won by the Communist Party, interrupted any sustained Confucian renewal in China. Of course, Korea and Japan had different fates. Korea was colonized by Japan and although Confucianism continued to play a role in Korean personal social life, it was only free to do so under Japanese official scrutiny. And although Japan sought to embrace all aspects of its past as part of Japanese cultural uniqueness, any truly critical thought was constrained by the growing power of the military in Japanese life. All virtues in Japan paled when contrasted to loyalty to the emperor and the growing Japanese empire.

After the Second World War, East Asia underwent yet another sea change. Japan, the most modernized country in the region, had been decisively defeated and much of its industrial infrastructure was destroyed. The military was completely rejected and other cultural props of the militarized state were abandoned. Of course, various facets of Confucianism were also criticized. Confucianism was perceived as being too willing to go along with the military's authoritarian practices. Even a relatively modernized Confucianism could not withstand the dark forces at work in Japanese culture that led to the destruction of the whole pre-war Japanese state.

However, after the communist revolution in China and the economic miracle in Japan, the situation began to change. In the first place, there was the empirical fact of the East Asian economic miracle – Sony radios and TVs, followed by Toyota cars flooded and even dominated many regions of the world, including North America. Japan rose from the ashes of defeat to become the second strongest economy in the world. Moreover, Japan was soon joined by South Korea, Taiwan, Hong Kong, and Singapore. The four smaller states were known as the mini-dragons due to their rapid industrialization.

All kinds of theories were invented to account for the rapid economic success of Japan, South Korea, Taiwan, Hong Kong, and Singapore. Some social scientists and historians began to ask if there was not an East

Asian model for modernization and industrialization, literally a second industrialization to match the industrial revolution of the West in the nineteenth and early twentieth centuries.

Pundits around the world asked, what do these dynamic East Asian economies and their supporting cultures have in common? One of the things that they all shared was a Confucian past. Suddenly there was a rush to look again at the Confucian heritage of East Asia, but this time in a radically transformed way. No longer was East Asia seen as backward and moribund. Rather, all of East Asia, and even China after the economic reforms of 1979, was now perceived as offering a different road to wealth and power than the one taken by the European and North Atlantic nations.

The new hypothesis was that Confucianism provided all kinds of useful and worthwhile cultural capital for the modernizing success of East Asia. The stress on the role of a stable family (even an extended family or large clan) – respect for education, reverence for the wisdom of age, a desire to promote the common good rather than to profess and practice an exaggerated individualism, a willingness to work hard, and an ability to defer instant gratification in order to promote future sustained growth, and more positive features – were attributed to the Confucian past of East Asian peoples. Confucianism was no longer part of the problem of cultural and economic backwardness, it was now part of the solution to all manner of social and cultural evils. Even the economic problems in Southeast and East Asia in the late 1990s paled in comparison to the general dynamic economic nature of the region.

The cultural future of Confucianism is less clear. All modern Confucians realize that they cannot restore a pristine version of the pre-modern past. Moreover, they also agree that this would not be right. There has always been a reforming, prophetic, or philosophic dimension to Confucianism that stretches back to Confucius and extends to the writings of the New Confucians. All of these texts concentrate on the need for reform of the person and society. It is always necessary to correlate the fundamental insights of the tradition with the contemporary scene. What is different today is the realization that Confucians live in a complex and modern world. The old desire for cultural and historical isolation, in fact, ignorance, of the rest of the world has disappeared from East Asia. It has been replaced by cultures that are seeking to be in tune with the best of their history and with the best of culture of the rest of the world. In the age of the internet, no other solution is possible.

What, then, will the New Confucianism look like? The first lesson of history is that it will take different shapes in China, Korea, Japan, Vietnam, and now places such as Singapore. Second, Confucianism is rapidly moving beyond the boundaries of East Asia. We have stressed that Confucianism was and is a multinational movement. Now it is becoming a global movement. This is happening because of two major factors. The first factor is the immigration of Chinese and East Asian people around the world. This has created a large and progressive East Asian diaspora, especially in North America. The second factor is that East Asians are no longer alone in thinking about the global nature of modern civilization. Confucianism and other forms of Asian philosophy and spirituality have arrived in the Western world at a time when the West itself is seeking new answers to old questions, and is hence receptive to reflections on what other cultures have to contribute to the new world order. It is clear that society in the future will not simply be Western in nature.

Although prophecy is dangerous when gazing into the future of any great tradition such as Confucianism, we are probably safe about making a few very general observations. The first has to do with the fundamental shape of the New Confucian movement. In the terms of one of its most able exponents, Professor Tu Weiming of Harvard University, Confucianism will remain an inclusive humanism. It is important to ponder the definition of "inclusive" humanism. The New Confucians believe that something like Mou Zongsan's notion of concern consciousness is a root metaphor for all the variegated manifestations of Confucian thought, personal cultivation, and social praxis. To be Confucian is to seek to be humane – to embody the fundamental virtue of *ren* or humaneness. But it is an inclusiveness that is now open to the cultural capital of the entire world. It is open to the glories of Bach and the romantic poets and the advanced scientific technology of Silicon Valley; it also fascinates, and is sometimes repelled, by debates about human rights and other Western philosophic and religious sensibilities. It is also open to the spiritual and religious dimension of human life. In short, it is a non-reductive, embracing form of humanism.

New Confucianism as a fundamental inclusive humanism will also, like all the other great religions of humankind, engage in a hermeneutic of retrieval, reformation, and transformation. The retrieval will seek out texts that can be read with profit in the modern world. Such texts as the famous *Four Books* will remain prime candidates for continued interest.

This holds for the internationalized Confucianism as well. Of course, other texts such as the *Classic of Changes*, the *Classic of Filial Piety*, and the *Book of Poetry* will also remain part of the domain of the hermeneutics of retrieval.

This process of modern Confucian education is only beginning afresh in China. However, Confucian studies have flourished in Taiwan, Hong Kong, Japan, and Korea since the Second World War. In Korea there is a prominent Confucian University. In Japan, critical scholarship has been the rule, and Japanese scholars continue to provide valuable insight into the history of the Confucian Way not only in Japan but also in the rest of East Asia. In Hong Kong, New Asia College, founded by famous New Confucian scholars after the communist revolution of 1949, has become an integral part of the Chinese University of Hong Kong.

Scholarly bookstores that would not have had a single positive book about Confucianism twenty years ago are now stocked with reprints and new editions of the Confucian classics. Beijing University, the premier university in China, has just published its own new, multivolume critical edition of the thirteen classics. Along with classical studies, new editions of great Neo-Confucians such as Zhu Xi and Wang Yangming have also appeared. And last, but not least, there are even special sections now devoted to the New Confucian movement. Titles about New Confucianism deal with its history, its art theory, its management techniques – and much more. There are even post-modern critical studies of Confucianism to be found among the shelves of classical texts.

THE INNER SAGE AND OUTER KING

One of the internal critiques of New Confucians, when they review the progress of the modern Confucian reformation, rests on the proper balance of theory and praxis. A famous Confucian metaphor used for defining the full ideal scope of the tradition is "sage within, king without." This means that the ideal Confucian ought to embody the highest ethical virtues along with a piety before learning and scholarship and a true form of intellectual discernment. However, this "inner" life of the sage must be conjoined with the "kingliness" without. The plethora of academic work being done in the universities of China and now the rest of the world speaks of the inner sage, the person of education and discernment. Of course, New Confucians are not advocating a revival of the old imperial system with an emperor at the helm of the Chinese state.

But they do accept the point that New Confucianism must articulate a viable modern social and political agenda that will speak convincingly to the mind-hearts of the people of East Asia.

Oddly, one area wherein there has been a positive model developed in which the Confucian tradition informs social praxis, is in business and management theory. One of the key elements of any ideal Confucian social order is social harmony, and one arena where this has been effective has been in the organization of business. For instance, the Japanese model of consensus management and internal dialogue has now been studied in the West. The Confucian contribution comes from the awareness that real harmony comes from the graceful adjustment of mutual needs, including frank discussions of differences. Although this effort at consensus building seems somewhat counterproductive in terms of Western styles of management, once sufficient time has been given over to debate, better and more productive working relations and actual manufacturing goals are achieved.

So while the business community in East Asia has never been perceived as a leader of the Confucian community, many enlightened businesspeople influenced by Confucianism are providing one example of concrete social policy founded on Confucian habits of the heart-mind. Of course, New Confucians realize that the appeal to social harmony can be a smokescreen for all kinds of other abuses by people in power. Another Confucian insight must also become part of Confucian business theory, namely a renewed vision of social justice. This is not at all hard to envisage because justice is one of the five fundamental Confucian virtues. Justice will balance the need for harmony with the needs for critical thinking and praxis. Confucians, from Confucius and Mencius to the most modern New Confucians, have understood that true human flourishing is only possible when all the five virtues are embedded in personal and social praxis.

It is fascinating to see how the Confucian-influenced business community is responding to the emerging paradigm of global business ethics. The new consensus is a bare minimum of three themes: a rejection of bribery, cronyism, and corruption as a natural way to do business; rejection of discrimination in the workplace based on race, religion, ethnicity, or gender; and a growing awareness of the need for a respect for the environment. In practice, these three new ethical norms challenge the Confucian tradition in terms of one interpretation of the notion of the "sage within, king without" model.

One of the critiques of the Confucian tradition is that this inner-outer distinction has been misused in concrete social situations. For instance, it is taken to mean that the inner circle of social relations beginning with the family and immediate social setting should take ethical precedence over the larger society, global community, and the common environment. However, New Confucians counter that this is a mistaken reading of the developmental stages of Confucian regard and respect for other persons. Whereas it is true that we all begin life in a family and must learn most of our ethics there, this is not to be interpreted as the claim that our fully developed ethics can only be practiced within the family. Actually, it is only when we can function ethically within the family that we can function effectively outside the family, and the connection between the inner and outer realms of social and ethical conduct can never be separated.

The reason for Confucian ethics to come into dialogue with the international business world is that the latter has become truly international in scope since the end of the Second World War. Japanese business leaders, because Japan was the first East Asian country to go international, had to realize that some of their ways of doing business violated good pragmatic norms for success along with some fundamental Confucian ethical injunctions. For instance, Japanese business leaders had developed a very cozy and interlocking way of doing business in Japan. This arrangement of banks, suppliers, manufacturers, and distributors mirrored the family structure. However, Japanese business leaders discovered that when they worked internationally, this tight circle of Japanese cooperation was viewed as closed and clannish. In ethical terms, the older Japanese way of doing business lacked a sense of fairness, and in fact, the term fair or fairness was mentioned more and more by leaders in the business community.

The Confucian ethical point was and is that we live in an interconnected world, a vast web of duties, opportunities, and responsibilities to oneself and others. Once a Confucian business has made contact with new businesses, it needs to expand its basic notion of fairness to include rather than exclude its new partners. To treat others without respect and justice violates the real norms of Confucian behavior. Much the same kind of discussion is now going on among Chinese business leaders both in China proper and the international Chinese world. In the Chinese case the problem had been too much reliance on individual family relations. There was a lack of trust towards anyone beyond the family itself; the New Confucians reminded the business leaders that their obligations toward their families could only truly be secured if, and only if, all of society flourished along with specific individuals. Fairness needed to be extended to all members of the business community.

Therefore, the ancient Confucian typology of the inner sage and external ruler does have a continuing significance even within the sphere of modern multinational business. In fact, Confucians argue that only when fairness is linked to harmony and respect for the person, can a really decent new world order be established. Of course, the details will differ, as one would expect, from visions of human flourishing as found in the Western tradition. However, there is so much borrowing going on between East and West these days that some of the older differences have disappeared. For instance, the continued struggle of the democracy movement in China and the recognition of a generalized human rights regime on the part of the New Confucian movement testifies to the spread of a global cultural discourse.

TWO BEGINNINGS IN QUFU

There is probably no better place to end the story of Confucianism than in Qufu, the hometown of the Master. According to tradition, 1999 marks the 2550th anniversary of the first sage, the teacher of the ten thousand generations. Like so many other cultural sites in China, Qufu suffered severe damage during the destructive rampages of the Cultural Revolution (at its worst from c. 1965 to the early 1970s). Qufu has remained the center of the Kong clan. The town is the site of the Confucian Temple, the Kong family mansion, and the large park known as the Confucian Forest. Reportedly, more than 100,000 members of the Kongs of Qufu have been buried here for the past 25 centuries. During the Cultural Revolution, the burial mounds of the Master and his descendants were desecrated. The only space, we are told, that was spared destruction, was the innermost sections of the Confucian Temple. Now major restoration work is underway in the Temple, Forest, and compound.

There is a new and impressive conference and research center under construction in Qufu as well. The conference center and library compound is grand and spacious. The centerpiece is a multistory library, exhibition space, and office building. It is thoroughly modern yet modeled after Song dynasty Chinese monumental architecture. The comparison with the boxy, Russian-style Great Hall of the People in Beijing is dramatic. In the foyer of the main hall is a four-story bas-relief copy of a famous Northern Song landscape painting. Under the relief are the life-size statues of Confucius and his four favorite disciples (see plate 4). The Master is standing and teaching; the four disciples are sitting and listening attentively. Somehow the ancient and the modern are fused together. One can only hope that the future of the Confucian Way will be as resplendent as the new research institute. That Confucius is being memorialized by the foundation of a research institute dedicated to Confucian studies is an appropriate and memorable way to begin the story of the Confucian tradition in a new century.

DYNASTIC AND INTELLECTUAL CHRONOLOGIES

	Fu Xi Shen Nong Huangdi Yao Shun Yu	Era of the Legendary Sage Kings and Empires
?–*c.* 1751 B.C.E. *c.* 1751–1045 1045–249	Xia Shang Zhou	The Three Eras of High Antiquity
1111–771 770–256 722–481 480–221	Western Zhou Eastern Zhou Spring and Autumn Warring States	
551–479 *c.* 385–312 *c.* 310–219	Confucius Mencius Xunzi	
221–206 206 B.C.E.–220 C.E.	Qin Han	The Imperial States
206 B.C.E.–9 C.E. 9–23 25–220	Western Han Xin Eastern Han	
c. 195–105 B.C.E.	Dung Chongshu	

220–65	Wei	Three
222–80	Wu	Kingdoms
221–63	Shu-Han	(220–80)
226–316	Western Jin	
317–420	Eastern Jin	The Period of
386–589	Northern and Southern Dynasties	Division (316–589)
420–79	Song	
479–502	Qi	
502–57	Liang	Southern (420–589)
557–89	Cheng	
386–534	Northern Wei	
534–50	Eastern Wei	
550–77	Northern Qi	Northern (386–581)
535–57	Western Wei	
557–81	Northern Zhou	
581–618	Sui	
618–907	Tang	
768–824	Han Yu	
907–23	Later Liang	
923–36	Later Tang	
936–47	Later Jin	Five Dynasties
947–50	Later Han	(907–960)
951–60	Later Zhou	
916–1125	Liao (North China)	
960–1127	Northern Song	Song
1127–1279	Southern Song	960–1279
1017–73	Zhou Dunyi	
1011–77	Shao Yong	
1020–77	Zhang Zai	
1032–85/ 1033–1107	Cheng Hao & Cheng Yi	
1130–1200	Zhu Xi	
1115–1234	Jin	
1260–1368	Yuan	

| 1472–1529 | Wang Yangming | ⎫ | Ming |
| 1578–1645 | Liu Zongzhou | ⎬ | (1368–1644) |

1644–1911	Qing
1619–92	Wang Fuzhi
1724–77	Dai Zhen

GLOSSARY

The *Book of Documents*	One of the early Confucian classics; considered basically a book of history and collection of historical records.
Bound feet	The practice of binding a young woman's feet in order to create an artificially small foot. The practice was painful, deforming, and unfortunately common from the Song dynasty to the end of the Qing period.
The Confucian Way/Dao	The specific path or way of Confucians; often thought of as "this culture of ours." To be distinguished from the Ways of Daoism and Buddhism.
Dao	The Way, the path of proper conduct; the matrix of all that is, moral, physical, and mortal.
Duke of Zhou (11th century B.C.E)	One of Confucius' great cultural heroes who secured the early fortunes of the Zhou dynasty. Brother of King Wu (see below).
Father Malipiero, S.J.	This is, of course, a fictitious Jesuit missionary. However, there were many learned Italian Jesuits active in the China mission at this time.
Fengshui	Literally means "wind and water." It is the ancient art of "siting" or the art of selecting auspicious sites for houses, gardens, tombs, temples, or any other building of substance.
Five phases or *wuxing*.	The five forms of *qi* or vital energy that are manifested in the world; fire, wood, water, earth, and metal. These should not be thought of as five distinct elements; rather they are the five phases of the vital force or energy of things. Used along with the concepts of yin and yang.

Four Books	The four classical Confucian texts, *The Great Learning, The Analects, The Mencius,* and *The Doctrine of the Mean,* selected by Zhu Xi to form the core of Confucian education from the Yuan dynasty to the end of the Qing dynasty in 1905.
The Great Learning	First of the Four Books and considered the gateway to the study of all the classics since the Southern Sung dynasty (1127–1279).
Han Yu (786–824)	Great Tang dynasty Confucian scholar; some credit him with the beginning of the Neo-Confucian revival completed in the Song dynasty.
Kami	Japanese term for the spirits of the indigenous Japanese religion of Shinto.
King Wen and King Wu (11th century B.C.E.)	The founders, father and son, of the Zhou dynasty and deemed by Confucius as sage kings.
Legalism/Legalists	One of the most important schools that contested with the Confucians during the Warring States period. They believed in the application of law to all aspects of life. Further, they denied that morality was important in government; people only respond to two basic drives, pain and pleasure. The Legalists have always been remembered as an evil force in Chinese life.
Li	The vast code of Confucian rituals that guided all forms of human life from birth to death. Best thought of as the form of civility between and among people.
Li	The form or patterns of the things and events of the world. One of the basic philosophic building blocks of Zhu Xi's system of thought; Zhu's thought was even often called *lixue* or the learning of principle.
Mencius (c. 371–289 B.C.E.)	The second of the great classical Confucian thinkers of the Zhou dynasty; memorialized as the Second Sage after Confucius.
Mind-heart or *xiu*	Classical Confucian thought always argued that the mind-heart included both reason and emotion, hence to call *xiu* the "mind" in English loses the emotional side of the Confucian understanding of discernment.
Mind-heart of Man	The passionate, emotional and uncultivated state of the human mind-heart before it is properly cultivated; our natural, undisciplined mind-heart.
Mind-heart of the Way	The manifestation of the Dao for perfected human emotion, thought, and action; the goal of self-cultivation.
Mozi	A great early philosophic critic of Confucianism; developed a sophisticated form of utilitarian ethics along with a rigorous logical system.

Qi	Often translated as vital force, matter-energy, vapor or a host of other terms. It is the protean 'stuff' out of which all things and events emerge and to which they return. The fundamental dynamic vital force of the cosmos.
Ren	Often translated as humanity, compassion or humaneness, this is the virtue of virtues for Confucians. Only a true sage manifests humaneness.
Ru	The most common Chinese term for the English term Confucian. No one is sure of its earliest meaning; however, it became the general name in the Zhou dynasty of the emerging class of experts and scholars of ritual.
Shinto	The original Japanese religious tradition before the arrival of Buddhism and Confucianism. Known for its respect for and veneration of nature.
Shogun/shogunate	The Japanese term for the military governments that ruled in the name of the Emperor. The last and most powerful of the Shoguns founded the Tokugawa regime in 1600; the Tokugawa ruled till 1868.
Shu	One of the ways Confucians describe the features of *ren* as empathy, a willingness to forgive others; benevolence.
Tael	A standard of Qing currency.
Taiji	The Supreme Ultimate; the highest form of principle. Everything that is has its own *taiji* and the Dao itself could be said to be the Supreme Ultimate of the cosmos itself.
Taiping (Rebellion)	A great quasi-Christian popular rebellion that devastated south and central China in the 1850s and 1860s. Perhaps causing more deaths than any other war in human history.
Tian	Literally the heavens; also refers to the high god of the Zhou ruling house. Often translated as heaven, however, it later came to lose its theistic connotations and came to mean the way the world really is.
Wang Yangming (1472–1529)	The great Ming dynasty philosopher of the mind-heart. His work challenged the thought of Zhu Xi and is considered second in influence only to Master Zhu in the formation of the Neo-Confucian tradition.
Xunzi (*c.* 310–210 B.C.E.)	The third of the great classical Confucians. The most systematic thinker of the group, he was considered a black sheep because he dared to contravene Mencius by teaching that human nature is evil.

Yangban	The traditional Korean term for the ruling aristocratic elite in Choson Korea (1392–1910).
Yin and yang	The basic polar forces or actions of the Dao; the forces of movement and quiet, warm and cold, hard and soft, etc. Everything that is has both yin and yang aspects.
Yamen Compound	The official office and staff of a magistrate, and all of local clerks, bailiffs; includes all the services of the government as well the local jail, etc.
Zhuangzi (*c.* 399–295 B.C.E.)	Greatest of the Zhou Daoist philosophers; renowned both for his philosophic brilliance and savage humor as well as his wonderful prose.
Zhu Xi (1130–1200)	The greatest of the Southern Song Neo-Confucian philosophers. The second most important Confucian thinker after Confucius himself. His works were the basis of the civil service examinations from 1313 to 1905.

BIBLIOGRAPHY

Allan, Sarah, 1991, *The Shape of the Turtle: Myth, Art, and Cosmos in Early China*, Albany, NY: State University of New York Press.

Ames, Roger T. and Rosemont, Henry, Jr., translators, 1998, *The Analects of Confucius: A Philosophical Translation*, New York: Ballantine Books.

Berthrong, John H., 1998, *Transformations of the Confucian Way*. Boulder, CO: Westview Press.

Blunden, Caroline and Elvin, Mark, 1991, *The Cultural Atlas of World: China*, Alexandria, VA: Stonehenge Press.

Chan, Wing-tsit, 1963, *A Source Book in Chinese Philosophy*, Princeton: Princeton University Press.

Ching, Julia, 1977, *Confucianism and Christianity: A Comparative Study*, Tokyo: Kodansha International.

Ching, Julia, 1993, *Chinese Religions*, Maryknoll, NY: Orbis Books.

Chu Hsi and Lü Tsu-ch'ien, 1967, *Reflections on Things at Hand: The Neo-Confucian Anthology*, trans. Wing-tsit Chan. New York: Columbia University Press.

Chu Hsi, 1991, *Chu Hsi's Family Rituals: A Twelfth-Century Chinese Manual for the Performance of Cappings, Weddings, Funerals, and Ancestral Rites*, trans. and ed. Patricia Buckley Ebrey, Princeton: Princeton University Press.

Fung, Yu-lan, 1952–53, *A History of Chinese Philosophy*, 2 Vols, trans. by Derk Bodde, Princeton: Princeton University Press.

Graham, A.C., 1989, *Disputers of the Tao: Philosophical Argument in Ancient China*, La Salle, IL: Open Court.

Grayson, James Huntley, 1989, *Korea: A Religious History*, Oxford: Clarendon Press.

Hoobler, Thomas and Hoobler, Dorothy, 1993, *Confucianism: World Religions*, New York: Facts On File.

Ivanhoe, Philip J., 2000, *Confucian Moral Self Cultivation*, second edition. Indianapolis, IN: Hackett Publishing Company, Inc.

Jochim, Christian, 1986, *Chinese Religions: A Cultural Perspective*, Englewood Cliffs, NY: Prentice-Hall.

Ko, Dorothy, 1994, *Teachers of the Inner Chambers: Women and Culture in Seventeenth-Century China*, Stanford: Stanford University Press.

Leys, Simon, trans. 1997, *The Analects of Confucius*, New York: W.W. Norton & Company.

Lopez, Donald S., Jr., 1996, *Religions of China in Practice*, Princeton, NY: Princeton University Press.

Lynn, Richard John, trans. 1994, *The Classic of Changes: A New Translation of the I Ching as Interpreted by Wang Bi*, New York: Columbia University Press.

Makra, Mary Lelia, trans. 1961, *The Hsiao Ching*, Edited by Paul K.T. Sih. New York: St. John's University Press.

Mann, Susan, 1997, *Precious Records: Women in China's Long Eighteenth Century*, Stanford, CA: Stanford Univerity Press.

Mote, F.W. 1999, *Imperial China: 900–1800*, Cambridge, MA: Harvard University Press.

Nakamura, Hajime, 1969, *A History of the Development of Japanese Thought from A. D. 592 to 1868*, Tokyo: Japan Cultural Society.

Paper, Jordan, 1995, *The Spirits are Drunk: Comparative Approaches to Chinese Religion*, Albany, NY: State University of New York Press.

Rozman, Gilbert (ed.), 1991, *The East Asian Region: Confucian Heritage and Its Modern Adaptation*, Princeton, NJ: Princeton University Press.

Schirokauer, Conrad, 1990, *A Brief History of Chinese Civilization*, Second edition. Fort Worth, TX: Harcourt Brace.

Schirokauer, Conrad, 1993, *A Brief History of Japanese Civilization*, Second edition. Fort Worth, TX: Harcourt Brace.

Schwartz, Benjamin I., 1985, *The World of Thought in Ancient China*, Cambridge, MA: The Belknap Press of Harvard University.

Sommer, Deborah, (ed.), 1995, *Chinese Religion: An Anthology of Sources*, New York and Oxford: Oxford University Press.

Spence, Jonathan D., 1974, *Emperor of China: Self-portrait of K'ang-hsi*, New York: Alfred A. Knopf.

Sung Tz'u, 1981, *The Washing Away of Wrong*, trans. Brian E. McKnight, Ann Arbor, MI: Center for Chinese Studies, The University of Michigan.

Taylor, Rodney L., 1990, *The Religious Dimensions of Confucianism*, Albany, NY: State University of New York Press.

Tu, Wei-ming, 1989, *Centrality and Commonality: An Essay on Confucian Religiousness*, Albany, NY: State University of New York Press.

Widmer, Ellen and Kang-I Sun Chang, eds, 1997, *Writing Women in Late Imperial China*, Stanford, CA: Stanford University Press.

Yang, C.K., 1967, *Religion in Chinese Society*, Berkeley: University of California Press.

Yao, Xinzhong, 2000, *An Introduction to Confucianism*. Cambridge: Cambridge University Press.

INDEX

Page numbers in *italic* indicate plates.

cultivation 35, 36, 84–5
definition 89
revolt, right of 49
Ricci, Matteo 139
righteousness (I) 89
ritual specialists (ru) 12–13, 48–9
rituals
Confucius on 86
family 81, 99, 162–4, 170–1
welcoming 166
rocks 146–7
rubbings 152
rulers
corrupt 28
filiality 58–60, 63, 64
mandate of heaven 49
Mencius on 14

'sage within, king without' model
185, 186–7, 188
sages 11–12, 29–30, 77, 80–2, 85–6
see also Duke of Zhou; King Wen;
King Wu
School of Han Studies see Evidential
Research School
School of Mind-heart (xinxue) 104,
156
School of Principle 104, 137, 156
School of the Way (Daoxue) 92–6,
97, 99
Second Sage see Mencius
Second Wave of Confucianism 21
Second World War 182
self-cultivation 14, 17–18, 25–42
back to the world 42
becoming a person 25–33
criminals 114
education 14, 33–4, 39, 55–64
emotions 102
field-focus metaphor 32
goals 31
meditation 30
mind-heart 136
quiet-sitting 33–42
ren 84–5
Wang Yangming on 34, 36–9, 42,
100–2
Zhang Zai on 95
Zhu Xi on 32–4, 36–8, 42, 97, 99
self-realization (cheng) 95
Shang dynasty 48, 49

Shao Yong 93–4
Shinto 177, 179
shoguns see Tokugawa shogunate
Shotoku, Prince 174
Sima Qian 16
Sima Tan 16
Singapore 182, 184
Sino-Japanese War (1895) 181
social ethics
Confucian Way 28
cultivation 29, 37–8, 95
education 57, 124
empathy 41–2, 62, 85
humaneness 12, 26, 33, 35–6, 62,
82–5, 184
principle 96
reciprocity 27, 39, 62, 84, 89
see also virtues
social harmony 18, 28–9, 31, 33, 85,
186
social order 87–8
Socrates 87
Song dynasty 18, 19–20, 59, 77
ceramics 152
Confucian texts 47, 53–4, 64
Confucian Way 20, 30, 32, 92–100
education system 56
fall 73
as Second Wave of Confucianism
21
Southern 73, 93, 96–100
see also Northern Song dynasty
Song Zu 109
South Asia 168
see also individual countries
South China 72–3
South Korea 182
Southern Song dynasty 73, 93,
96–100
see also Zhu Xi
Spinoza, Baruch 30
spread of Confucianism 4–7, 22,
138–9, 167–88
statecraft 35–6, 45–6
stones 146–7
The Strict Father Model 27
studies, furnishing 145–53
Su Shi 133
superstition 10, 84, 128
Supreme Ultimate 96, 98, 99, 135
Suzhou 2, 8, 9, 115–16